YOU ALWAYS HAVE A CHOICE

JULIE HYDE

YOU
Always
HAVE A
CHOICE

Embrace change, build unwavering resilience and **lead a life you love**

'A story of inspirational courage and resilience, Julie's book is a personal letter to the reader with a deep message of encouragement that will challenge you to quit making excuses and start living the life you want. A powerful process with the tools to enable you to look at yourself in the mirror every day and know if you've cheated that person looking back at you.'

– *Catherine Duncan, Partner and Chief Operating Officer*

'Julie Hyde is not only a fabulous writer but her lessons are key for us to hear. She faced an unwanted and difficult challenge and has real wisdom to share on what we can all do to make choices for the life we want. I loved the simple-to-follow messages and practical advice she has synthesised for us to focus on. This book will help all of us navigate any challenge with power, showing us how to have choice in our response and clear values to guide us.'

– *Dr Amy Silver, Psychologist, Speaker, Author*

'Julie is the real deal. Her vulnerability, positivity and practical guidance is the perfect recipe for real change. With so much rhetoric around choice and mindset, Julie, through her own incredibly inspiring story of strength, resilience and determination, provides useful and practical steps to truly take control of whatever is going on, and change your life. Julie's incredible career and ability to reinvent herself, personally and professionally, is leadership in living colour. *You Always Have a Choice* is a must-read for anyone looking for proven, real and authentic guidance from an inspired leader and beautiful human.'

– *Karen Matthews, CEO, Non-Executive Board Member and NSW Telstra Business Woman of the Year*

'A true journey of self-awareness and self-leadership from the inside out. A comprehensive, powerful guide and reminder that the power of choice is yours and yours to own.'

— *Melissa Williams, Head of Marketing and Fundraising*

'I'm sure we all have those moments where we feel as though we are simply going through the motions. I know I certainly have. When we find ourselves in these situations, we must always remember we can choose change. In fact, we must make this choice. This book outlines some questions we can ask ourselves and provides tips to help us have the confidence to put ourselves first. We all want to live life to the full. If you are searching for ways to get back the control, and still live life to the full, then this book might be just the tonic.'

— *Louise Baxter, CEO, Starlight Children's Foundation*

'Julie's book is engaging and practical, full of valuable information for those of us who wish to lead and make strong choices in our lives. Her lived experience demonstrates the effectiveness of the strategies discussed. I feel like I now have the strategies to make empowered choices and the strategies to implement them. A must-read.'

— *Michelle Bridgeman, Office Manager*

'*You Always Have a Choice* provides a roadmap to seize control in life's whirlwind. Julie's profound insights are an empowering beacon for those in search of balance and resilience. An essential read for anyone craving inspiration during tough times.'

— *Carlo Pagano, General Regional Manager*

To my Dad – thank you for being my greatest role model and for your unwavering belief in me.

I miss you every day.

First published in 2024 by Julie Hyde

© Julie Hyde 2024
The moral rights of the author have been asserted

All rights reserved. Except as permitted under the *Australian Copyright Act 1968* (for example, a fair dealing for the purposes of study, research, criticism or review), no part of this book may be reproduced, stored in a retrieval system, communicated or transmitted in any form or by any means without prior written permission.

All inquiries should be made to the author.

A catalogue entry for this book is available from the National Library of Australia.

ISBN: 978-1-92300753-6

Printed in Australia by Pegasus
Book production and text design by Publish Central
Cover design by Pipeline Design

The paper this book is printed on is certified as environmentally friendly.

Disclaimer: The material in this publication is of the nature of general comment only, and does not represent professional advice. It is not intended to provide specific guidance for particular circumstances and it should not be relied on as the basis for any decision to take action or not take action on any matter which it covers. Readers should obtain professional advice where appropriate, before making any such decision. To the maximum extent permitted by law, the author and publisher disclaim all responsibility and liability to any person, arising directly or indirectly from any person taking or not taking action based on the information in this publication.

CONTENTS

Introduction		1
Chapter 1	Overwhelmed? You're in the Right Place	7
Chapter 2	Pushing the Pause Button	21
Chapter 3	The Power of Choice	35
Chapter 4	Embracing Change, Big or Small	51
Chapter 5	Your Mindset is Your Superpower	71
Chapter 6	Building Your Resilience	89
Chapter 7	Have the Courage to be the CEO of You	107
Chapter 8	Drawing a Line in the Sand	123
Chapter 9	Success on Your Terms	137
Conclusion		151
About the Author		155
Acknowledgements		157
References		159

INTRODUCTION

Many people I speak with professionally and personally are feeling overwhelmed. The relentlessness of life often takes us to our capacity point, where we feel we've had enough. Life is too short to constantly feel that way.

When Penny contacted me, she felt trapped and fed up. Her life didn't align with her desires and she sensed that it was slipping out of her control. She was going through the motions, exhausted by the constant struggle and not truly living. Deep down, Penny knew she needed a change but a lack of confidence and energy held her back. She found herself at a crucial crossroads – having to choose whether to stick with what's familiar or to boldly take steps towards a life she truly loved. It wasn't an easy choice but one she needed to make.

I could relate to her struggle because I've been in that place numerous times, and so too have many of my clients. Misalignment and overwhelm are common experiences in people's lives. It's easy to lose sight of what truly matters when we're driven to constantly improve and achieve. But what's the point of all of that if it doesn't lead to genuine happiness?

The poignant words of writer Dale Wimbrow in his poem, 'The Guy in the Glass', reflects this beautifully. As you read it you might imagine it's written just for you:

> *When you get what you want in your struggle for pelf,*
> *And the world makes you King for a day,*
> *Then go to the mirror and look at yourself,*
> *And see what that guy has to say.*
>
> *For it isn't your Father, or Mother, or Wife,*
> *Who judgement upon you must pass.*
> *The feller whose verdict counts most in your life*
> *Is the guy staring back from the glass.*
>
> *He's the feller to please, never mind all the rest,*
> *For he's with you clear up to the end,*
> *And you've passed your most dangerous, difficult test*
> *If the guy in the glass is your friend.*
>
> *You may be like Jack Horner and 'chisel' a plum,*
> *And think you're a wonderful guy,*
> *But the man in the glass says you're only a bum*
> *If you can't look him straight in the eye.*
>
> *You can fool the whole world down the pathway of years,*
> *And get pats on the back as you pass,*
> *But your final reward will be heartaches and tears*
> *If you've cheated the guy in the glass.*

As he touchingly says, the last person you want to be cheating is you, and the most important person you need to be happy with is the person who is looking back at you from the mirror.

I want this book to release your pressure valve. I hope reading it is like heading out for coffee or wine with your closest, most inspirational friend who only wants the best for you and encourages you to thrive. I hope it gives you the space to breathe and to feel a sense of calm, while also reassuring you that you are not alone in how you're feeling.

Life is an ever-flowing river of opportunities and constant change. Change is one of the things we can count on. It embodies choice itself. Whether we face change with resistance, resentment or open arms is entirely up to us – regardless of whether it's welcomed or not.

> **LIFE'S UNPREDICTABILITY MEANS WE CAN'T ALWAYS CONTROL WHAT HAPPENS TO US, BUT WE HOLD THE POWER TO CONTROL OUR RESPONSES.**

But how do we do that? We all need practical strategies to apply to life's challenges, and that is what this book is about.

Throughout my life, I've encountered a multitude of changes. Spending 21 years in the corporate world exposed me to big changes happening every two years or so, be it organisational change or shifts in job roles. But one day I made the decision that altered everything. I chose to start my own business, to be my own boss. This transition was massive, transforming how I operated and changing me into the person I needed to become.

In the 16 years since, I've worn various hats as a leadership coach, keynote speaker and podcast host. To stay relevant in this ever-changing landscape, I've continually evolved and adapted. Not only have I embraced universal and technological changes, but I've also kept a close eye on my clients' evolving demands and needs.

Then, in October 2021, I experienced what was to be the biggest change to my life so far. I received a shock diagnosis of aggressive stage three melanoma cancer. As someone who had always been fit and healthy and who loved to be in control, I was shell-shocked.

Now I had the biggest opportunity of my life to test all of the theories and practices I had developed over the years. This change tested me and my mindset – and, to this day, it presents constant challenges that require me to change and adapt. But I could rely on the one thing I knew to be true: my mindset is my superpower. I was confident in that and the bucketload of resilience that I could dig into. I find strength in knowing that change, no matter how daunting, holds the key to growth and endless possibilities. I'll be showing you how to strengthen your mindset and embrace those possibilities, too.

> YOU HOLD THE POWER OF CHOICE TO LEAD A LIFE YOU LOVE.

You can adapt to change and build your resilience and confidence to be happy, feel fulfilled and be proud of yourself. You can make the choice to move away from overwhelm and juggling unnecessary expectations to be truly happy. You always have a choice, no matter what.

The art of choice is at the heart of this book. It's about mastering the skill of making empowered decisions that align with who you are and what you dream of. Within these pages, I'll introduce you to nine powerful strategies that have transformed lives, including my own and those of countless clients. You'll also get to explore not

INTRODUCTION

one but two game-changing business models that open doors to the power of choice and cultivate a superpower mindset.

Simplicity is our ally here. This book is all about making things easy to grasp and enticing to read. There is no technical jargon or bland instructions. I've filled this book with actionable insights and real-world examples.

Building your confidence, finding your voice and cultivating resilience will become second nature. With these invaluable tools in your kit, you'll tackle any future change head-on and emerge stronger and even more resilient. By the time you reach the last page, your mindset will truly be your superpower. Mindset matters more than you can imagine, and I'll show you precisely why as we delve deeper.

Let's dive right in together.

Chapter 1

OVERWHELMED? YOU'RE IN THE RIGHT PLACE

On 6 October 2021, at approximately 7.30pm, I was diagnosed with stage three melanoma cancer. I was told it was aggressive, and that I was in for the fight of my life.

At that moment, I felt like I was on the downward slope of a steep and very scary roller-coaster. I could see my life rushing past. I wondered, is this the end? Am I going to die? Will my life be cut short right here, at 53?

The diagnosis completely turned my life upside down.

Within only five days, I'd had major surgery to remove the melanoma from the arch of my right foot. This was the melanoma's starting point. It then spread to the lymph nodes in my right groin area. They removed most of these, as they were full of cancer.

When I woke up after four hours of surgery, I had a 30 centimetre wound from my stomach down to the top of my right thigh. I had a hole in my foot bigger than a 50-cent piece that was covered by a skin graft. I had a wound on my left leg where they'd taken the skin for the skin graft. I was hooked up to various machines pumping painkillers and antibiotics into me, and others that were grinding away to help me heal. I was pretty banged up and in very unfamiliar territory. I was immobilised, unwell and felt very vulnerable – and I didn't like it.

> **REALITY IS SOMETIMES A TERRIBLE SHOCK. IT WAS IN MY CASE. BUT IT CAN ALSO BE YOUR BEST ASSET IN HELPING TO SHIFT UNWELCOME CHANGE FROM PAINFUL TO TRANSFORMATIVE.**

Facing reality means confronting the facts of your circumstances; in my case, the horrible diagnosis. I didn't want to accept my reality at all. I was in total denial and I kept wishing this wasn't happening to me. While I was trying to be brave in front of others, I was feeling scared inside.

We often live in denial, hoping life will get better. Denial can affect personal relationships and health, and lead to addictions and societal issues. You may deny your own shortcomings, avoid facing the consequences of your actions, or refuse to acknowledge the severity of a situation. This may create a false sense of security, but it stops personal growth and prevents you from solving challenges. It can hold you in a precarious position.

When the denial bubble bursts, you may feel shocked and overwhelmed. I have seen this play out in my life, and in the lives of my coaching clients, again and again. Even after my surgery, I was living in denial. I hoped that this was it and I wouldn't need further treatment. I wanted to return to my life pre-diagnosis. I wanted to be Julie before the cancer. But that was not my reality. My bubble burst quickly. When that happened, I felt very overwhelmed.

Overwhelm can be a natural response to situations that feel like they're too much to handle. This limit is different for everyone. Overwhelm can also be our own doing, when we find ourselves juggling too many balls and exceeding our capacity. In fact, I felt quite overwhelmed while writing this book!

Accepting your reality is key to reducing overwhelm. Doing so can provide critical insights for improvement and will help you adapt to change. Using your reality as an asset involves making informed decisions by recognising both the positive and the negative aspects of a situation. Proactively shaping your reality boosts your ability to create a life you love.

So many people are feeling overwhelmed. In this instance I'm not talking about an overwhelm that is too intensive to overcome or that paralyses you. I'm talking about the feeling of having too many tabs open in your brain, feeling stuck or trapped and living out of alignment with who you are, which leads to feeling unhappy. You might feel like it would be catastrophic if you dropped one of the balls you're juggling. You might feel exhausted, like you're running on a treadmill to nowhere. Or you might constantly feel worried that you're not pleasing anyone or succeeding at anything, while neglecting to look after yourself. It may be a combination of all three that's causing your overwhelm.

It's only when you take responsibility for the cause of your overwhelm that you have any chance of adapting and changing. This is especially true when you're accepting a situation you have no control over rather than one you have created. There is a moment of truth and wisdom when you accept what you might change.

In this chapter, we'll look at how the modern way of living life at full pelt, in a state of constant busyness, has a tremendous impact on our wellbeing. We'll evaluate the effects of being constantly on the go, and identify the underlying causes of being caught in the cycle of busyness – because if you're not busy, then who are you? We're going to explore the fact that you're not alone. Feeling overwhelmed is normal, and is often due to universal worries and an excessive mental load from our own and others' unrealistic expectations. It can also be a product of our own thoughts and actions. I'm also going to share with you that the juggle is real, but we have a choice in what we take on and how we respond. This part is important, because we're always going to be juggling many, many balls in the air. That's what's called life.

I'm then going to take you through an empowering exercise called labelling the balls. By labelling the balls, you will understand how many balls you are juggling and then decide how many balls you would *like* to juggle. You'll learn to identify which balls you can let bounce, and which balls you might never pick up again.

> 66 YOU HAVE THE POWER TO CHANGE YOUR LIFE AT ANY MOMENT, NO MATTER WHAT, AND THAT IS EXCITING.

LIFE AT FULL PELT

We are living life at full pelt. We are constantly busy. There's so much coming at us and there's always so much to do. Our metaphorical to-do list is never-ending. Recognising the constant busyness and its impact on your wellbeing is the key to being able to change. You need to evaluate the effects of being constantly on the go. You must identify the underlying causes of being caught in the cycle of busyness. There's a fine tipping point between a good, productive busy to a completely overwhelmed busy.

Let's clarify the distinction between these two states. The dictionary definition of 'busy' is 'having a great deal to do'. 'Good' busy is not just a chaotic whirlwind of activity. It signifies purposeful action that is aligned to your values, priorities and goals. It's not just doing things for the sake of doing them, or to please others. When you're 'good' busy you feel you're in control. You're getting things done but you also have time to reflect, rest and recharge your batteries. Being 'good' busy is approaching your day like an athlete would: making sure you're doing things that get you closer to achieving your goals and living the life you love.

Being 'bad' busy is characterised by feeling overwhelmed and that your tasks are insurmountable, feeling constantly tired or stressed, having difficulty relaxing even when your tasks are done, feeling like you are constantly playing catch-up and feeling out of control. You are constantly tethered to technology, whether that be looking at your emails or at your social media. You are most likely running on adrenaline. When you're not doing something productive, you feel guilty. Ultimately, you've become a human doing rather than a human being.

I discussed the difference between productive and reactive busy in my first book, *Busy*, which you can refer to for more detail.

There is a fine line between in control and out of control. As we go through life, depending on our situation – often what's happening in our home or our work environment – our capacity to handle what is going on changes. We need to adapt. A simple example of that is when you are feeling unwell with a cold or virus. This reduces your capacity to handle what life throws at you due to your low energy. Or it could be experiencing the loss of a loved one, a significant relationship, or a cherished aspect of your life such as your health or finances. All of this can reduce your ability to adapt. The overwhelming emotions and sense of emptiness can make it challenging to cope with life's changes and adjust to a new reality.

This book is going to show you how to adapt. It's about having the ability to flex so that when situations happen to you, you can change, adapt and get back in control quickly.

Being in a state of 'bad' busyness can lead to health concerns and burnout. By understanding the distinction between 'good' and 'bad' busy, you can choose which state of busy you operate in.

> IT'S MY DREAM TO BAN THE WORD 'BUSY'!
> I BELIEVE IT'S A HABITUAL STATE THAT WE OFTEN
> BELIEVE WE NEED TO OPERATE IN TO BE SUCCESSFUL.

The era of busyness has emerged as a relatively recent phenomenon. In the past, time was determined by natural phenomena such as the sun's movement and the ebb and flow of the seasons. The precision of timekeeping and clocks only unfolded in the 18th century, marking the beginning of our meticulous pursuit of time.

Concerns about busyness became widespread in the mid-20th century. Introducing the atomic clock in the 1950s allowed time to be measured with unprecedented accuracy down to the nanosecond. This newfound precision increased stress levels worldwide.

Hans Selye, a pioneer in stress science, embarked on important research during the mid-1940s. His work established the bedrock of stress science, highlighting the insidious effects of chronic stress on the human body. Selye's findings show the consequences of overwork.

The Cult of Busy, as termed by Johns Hopkins researchers, is alive and well today. Our culture celebrates being constantly busy, with grown-ups and kids alike having tight schedules all day long. Success is now equated with the degree of your busyness. Consequently, there is an incessant need to fill every waking moment, pushing the boundaries of human endurance.

The pervasive influence of the Cult of Busy has permeated all parts of our life. Burnout has become a common occurrence in the workplace. It has infiltrated our personal lives, where we often measure our self-worth by the level of our busyness and how many balls we can juggle.

You might think, 'I've got three kids, a full-time career, two dogs, a partner and a mortgage. I am busy because that's how I have to be.' Yes, but are you in control of your busyness or is your busyness controlling you? Identify your state of being right now. Take a moment to sit comfortably and close your eyes. Picture your typical day from when you wake up to when you go to bed. Take note of your activities, feelings and state of mind during the day. Consider the definitions that I shared with you before and label your state of being. Do you feel that you're busy and productive, or do you feel that you're busy and overwhelmed? You might struggle to do this exercise because you think, 'I am fine with being busy. I love being busy. I want to be busy.'

> **CONSIDER THIS: IF YOU WEREN'T BUSY, WHAT WOULD YOU CHOOSE TO BE DOING WITH YOUR TIME?**

YOU ARE NOT ALONE

Overwhelm is a common occurrence, closely related to feeling stuck or trapped. Overwhelm can be caused by global issues such as epidemics, environmental issues and political instability. There's a lot that happens universally that can put pressure on you and that is outside of your control. It can feel like nothing is going right and that there is no good news out there. Your social media feeds are flooded with chaos. It permeates the media you consume. When external changes land on your doorstep, you rarely feel like you've got the capacity to accommodate it. People felt overwhelmed when the pandemic hit. Regulations kept changing, making it too much to deal with. They hit capacity limits.

If you're feeling overwhelmed, you're not alone. The feeling is natural when things get too much. Don't add to your worries by feeling you're alone or being hard on yourself, thinking, 'I know better. I should be able to get over this overwhelm. I shouldn't feel this way.' I can assure you, having coached hundreds of people and spoken with thousands through my work, the feeling of overwhelm is common. It's felt on different scales and presents uniquely for each person, but it's common.

My cancer diagnosis was a huge situation that I could not control, even though I desperately wanted to. I felt very overwhelmed. I had my business that I needed to keep going. I had clients that I still wanted to service. I had a podcast that I was hosting. I had a life that I wanted to maintain. Initially, I wanted to keep all of those things going. But, of course, I couldn't.

My client Sarah had a demanding full-time job and was juggling a lot of balls. Sarah contacted me because she felt very overwhelmed. She felt like life had consumed her and she couldn't work her way through it to make it better. When I sat down with Sarah and we worked through the underlying causes of her overwhelm, it came down to the fact that she was juggling an unrealistic number of balls. She was very busy. Busy had become a habit. Sarah was used to living her life this way. Unknowingly, she was running on adrenaline and this had become addictive for her – until she hit her point of capacity. Sarah had put so many expectations on her own shoulders to make sure that she excelled at work. She loved riding on the weekend and spending time with friends. She was there for her kids and her husband. There was a lot she was doing. Sarah was unclear about her priorities and had no firm boundaries in place to ensure she lived in alignment with her goals. She had lost connection to who she was – what her values were and the type of person she wanted to be. Sarah was playing out something that a lot of us do.

Sarah and I worked out what was a realistic juggle for her and what balls she could drop for now. She realised she couldn't do everything all at once. Sound familiar? Yes, Sarah had several obligations that had to be met, but she was also doing tasks that were out of obligation rather than necessity. She caused some of her own overwhelm. When she got back in control of the juggle and created a life that she loved, she was back in the game. She felt more energised, resilient and able to deal with what life might have in store for her.

You might be thinking, 'I've always been capable, so what's different? Why am I feeling like I can't cope at the moment when I *can* cope at other times?' That's exactly how Sarah felt. She couldn't understand why she was feeling the way she did. She's very capable and self-aware. I reassured her, as I'm reassuring you, that sometimes we take on too much and try to do everything at once without even realising it. We can start living out of alignment with our values and what's important to us. We become disconnected from our inner feelings or ignore them. We persist with the same habits, feeling the same way.

If you're feeling overwhelmed to the point that you feel paralysed or depressed, try the ideas in this book. If you're still stuck, seek professional help and then come back to it.

To understand whether you are taking on too much or causing your own overwhelm, take a moment to reflect on how long you have been feeling like you have. Go for a walk and think about it. Take yourself away from the busyness and give yourself space. Often that will then allow you to think about how long this feeling has been permeating your life. When was the last time you didn't feel overwhelmed? Write it down. This may be challenging; realising how stressed or overwhelmed you feel can be uncomfortable and make you feel worse. Sit with this for as long as you need to feel the reality of your circumstances. This is important if you want to change or break your overwhelm and turn unresourceful busyness into resourceful, aligned productivity.

THE JUGGLE IS REAL

We'll always be juggling balls. That's life! Understanding why you choose to juggle so many balls can become your best asset. It gives you the power to decide how many balls you keep juggling and which to put down. I'm going to show you how labelling the balls gives you the power to change your life at any moment, no matter what. That's what this book is all about.

When I talk about juggling balls, I'm referring to all the responsibilities and expectations that you've taken on – whether by choice or necessity. It's a metaphorical juggling of tasks. Understanding you have a choice in how many balls you juggle – understanding your reality – provides you a starting point for change. Often, we don't think about what we *choose* to take on. We do things out of a misguided sense of obligation.

The first step is to label the balls, and it is a great exercise to start the journey. Brian Dyson, the former CEO of Coca-Cola, originally shared this concept at his commencement speech at Georgia Tech University in 1991. He said:

> *Imagine life as a game in which you are juggling some five balls in the air. You name them work, family, health, friends and spirit. And you're keeping these in the air.*
>
> *You will soon understand that work is a rubber ball. If you drop it, it will bounce back. But the other four balls – family, health, friends and spirit – are made of glass. If you drop one of these, they will be irrevocably scuffed, marked, nicked, damaged or even shattered. They will never be the same. You must understand that and strive for balance in your life.*

Very wise words.

I have adapted his wisdom slightly, and created three types of balls that we juggle:

1. *Crystal ball:* A precious ball that will shatter if dropped. It's a critical responsibility to keep in the air.
2. *Rubber ball:* This ball can bounce, and will keep bouncing until you pick it up again. It's important, but if it's dropped, it's not catastrophic. It's a choice to juggle this ball.
3. *Concrete ball:* A ball that feels heavy. Perhaps you are juggling it begrudgingly or to please someone else. Maybe it isn't critical to what you want to achieve. You might be juggling it out of habit. You can drop this ball and leave it on the ground.

Your challenge is to label all the balls you have in the air (see figure 1). Take a moment now to write each one down in a journal or on sticky notes. Define each ball as crystal, rubber or concrete. Yes, all of them! Once you have an accurate picture you will then know exactly where you are at. Now I encourage you to select a few concrete and/or rubber balls and let them drop. You can do it! When you drop them, feel some of that overwhelm melt away.

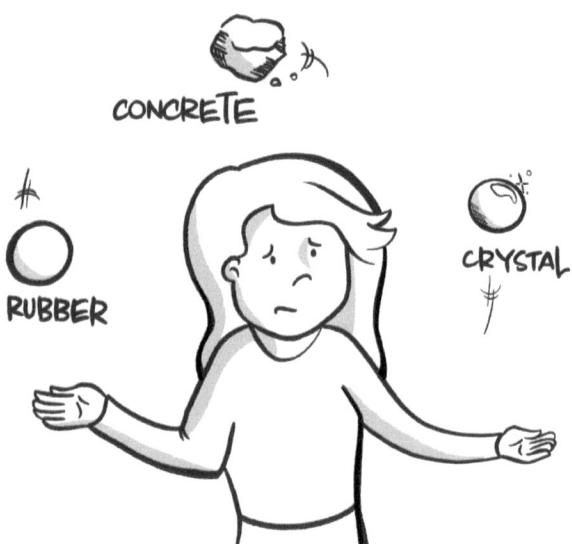

Figure 1: Defining the balls you're juggling

Labelling the balls you are juggling is important; it gives you the power to decide and prioritise what you choose to juggle. You also get a visual sense of your reality. It provides permission to drop some balls. I firmly believe that we can drop balls we're juggling and leave them dropped. And remember, not all balls are crystal!

You may not juggle all your balls today, but you could pick them up tomorrow, depending on what happens. This removes or reduces the feeling of guilt about letting a ball drop, or at least makes it easier.

You might think, 'I can't drop any balls. They are all crystal and I don't feel like I can. Every time I drop one, another one comes along and it becomes crystal.' I challenge you to drop one ball and let one bounce and see if it makes a difference. It's not easy, I understand that. But as you practise, prioritising crystal balls and letting others drop will become second nature.

CONCLUSION

In this chapter, you've learned that you are not alone and you are far from a failure if you're feeling overwhelmed. The weight of living at full pelt is a shared experience, a universal struggle that we all face. You've recognised the difference between being busy and in control as opposed to busy and overwhelmed. You have shown courage by analysing the frequency and source of your overwhelm. This self-awareness is now your lantern in the darkness, illuminating the path towards change.

No matter how many balls you juggle, remember this: you possess the power of choice. Each ball represents a responsibility, a commitment or a demand. By labelling them, you reclaim control over your life's rhythm. You make an empowered decision about which balls to release and which to keep juggling. Stop thinking that feeling overwhelmed is just how life is. It's not. Start making empowered decisions about how you live your life. Start believing that there is hope for you to turn this around.

In the next chapter, I will show you how to extend your self-reflection even deeper. By further embracing your situation, you can make the adaptive changes that you need.

Chapter 2

PUSHING THE PAUSE BUTTON

As counterintuitive as it sounds, when you are busy and overwhelmed the most important step is to pause momentarily. This is so you can assess the current situation; to take stock of which balls you're juggling and whether they are aligned to living a life you love. The concept of pausing will be a foundation that you build on in the other adaptive strategies that are coming up in this book. Pausing in this context means taking a moment to stop, breathe, think and reflect. It's a key part of the many strategies that I will share with you, and I promise you will learn to love the power of the pause.

I'm not talking about taking a huge chunk of time out of your day. I understand that might seem unmanageable or even impossible for you. I mean simply hitting pause with the intention of coming back to your other priorities later. I liken it to pushing the pause button on the remote control when you're watching an engrossing series or a good movie – when you think you'll miss out on too much of the storyline if you get up and make yourself a cup of tea or take a bathroom break. You can hit pause and come back to your show without having missed a second.

> **YOU CAN ALSO PUSH THE PAUSE BUTTON ON YOUR LIFE.**

This concept is key to help you increase your self-awareness and gain control of your life. It allows you to break the nasty cycle of busy and overwhelm. It's effective both personally and professionally. In fact it improves your performance.

A study revealed that employees who dedicated just 15 minutes at the conclusion of their workday to reflect on their experiences and lessons learned exhibited a remarkable 23 per cent improvement in performance over a span of ten days, compared to those who didn't engage in this reflective practice.[1]

In this chapter, I will show you what pushing the pause button looks like, why you want to embrace it as an awesome adaptive strategy, and how it can help unmask underlying patterns that are leading to overwhelm.

UNDERSTANDING HOW TO PAUSE

Pausing is something that you will use intentionally as you work through this book. I'm going to show you how you can introduce the practice of pausing each day. Pausing intentionally each day is important. It will prevent you from hitting a wall and being forced to stop.

One of the most beautiful things about being on holiday is the feeling of having time to do what you love. You have time to 'smell the roses', and often get a different perspective on things when you are on holidays. You've taken a pause in your working life to enjoy some rest and relaxation or experience a new culture. It's something that will help you to reset and rejuvenate yourself. This is the power of a pause. You can have a similar experience each day when you make it a regular practice.

Pausing to reflect is important. It gives your brain a break from life's chaos. It gives you the opportunity to sort through what has occurred during your day and make meaning of it. This then allows you to learn from your day – what went well and what didn't go so well. The insights can influence your future mindset and help you operate in a way that you're proud of. It also gives you the opportunity to consider if you are above or below the line (I will explain this concept in chapter 3).

If you don't pause, you will continue in your cycle of busyness, juggling balls you don't need to. You will become increasingly overwhelmed, eventually hitting a wall and potentially becoming ill. It might take a couple of months or a couple of years, but the consequences could be dire. Just think of the people you've heard about who have changed their lives because they received a serious health diagnosis. It's amazing what you can do when you have to. I always encourage people to pause before it becomes critical so they can avoid situations like that.

I recommend a daily pause to all my clients. It's also something that I do religiously at the end of each day. I carve out 15 minutes and ask myself the following three questions:

1. How was I as a leader today?
2. What did I do well?
3. What can I improve so that tomorrow is even better than today?

It's as simple as that. I'll then plan my following day and identify the mindset I need to adopt for it to be successful.

You might think, 'I seriously do not have time to pause.' I would like to hit this excuse on the head right now, early on in this book. Lack of time is not an excuse for anything. We are all equal in time. Regardless of affluence, culture and gender, we all have 24 hours, or 1440 minutes, or 86,400 seconds in the day. It's how you choose to use your time that matters. I'd also like to make something clear here: you will do what you prioritise. If you prioritise busy, you'll be busy. If you prioritise exercise, you will exercise. It depends on what you are prioritising. If you prioritise pushing the pause button, you will push the pause button. Time is not an excuse for not doing something.

I have a simple five-step strategy that you can implement to start your practice of pausing:

1. Choose a time in your day when you will press the pause button.
2. Decide on the length of time for your pause. Start small and build up so that you can achieve success with this. Maybe start with two minutes if it's a new practice for you, or longer if it's something that you are familiar with.
3. When you carve out this time, you will be by yourself. Ideally, you'll be outside, but that's not a deal-breaker.
4. Avoid sitting in front of your computer or being tethered to your phone.
5. It will be quiet around you.

This is your pause.

You might think, 'I'm never by myself. I've always got my kids or my partner around. There's always noise, the TV is always on.'

Maybe try taking your pause in the shower, while you're cleaning your teeth or when you are getting ready for bed. There *will* be a time in your day when you have silence. You might need to think hard about when that is.

UNLOCKING THE POWER OF A PAUSE

Pressing the pause button is a self-reflection tool that increases your self-awareness, especially in times of challenge or change. Self-reflection acts as a mirror, allowing you to examine your conscious and unconscious choices. It's a foundation to understand what you need to change or implement to avoid overwhelm, adapt to change and build resilience.

Self-awareness has many benefits. It helps you to self-regulate; it allows you to respond to change, challenge or crisis and interact with others and yourself much more effectively. The more self-aware you are, the more successful you are. Pushing the pause button will facilitate this for you.

Life and business will always throw curveballs our way. It doesn't take a severe health diagnosis like mine or something as extreme as a pandemic to turn your life upside down. We experience change constantly on both small and large scales. By pausing, you can understand what you need to adapt to. It's the same as when a crisis pops up – whether it be that your child is sick and you can't attend an important meeting, or the death of a loved one where your world stops on its axis for a time. It doesn't matter what the situation, pausing is the key to avoiding overwhelm.

Pausing allows for a shift in perspective. It provides the mental space needed to gain clarity. It allows you to examine your thoughts, behaviours and motivations, gaining important insights. This new-found clarity becomes a catalyst for change, empowering you to make decisions aligned with your values, goals and the life you want to lead.

My client Kane was referred to me by his leader because he wasn't performing at his full potential. A strong feeling of being overwhelmed had overtaken him. Kane was an executive in a large organisation. He had a team of 20 people. He handled sales, service, delivery, compliance and culture. It was a big role. He was also a dad of five active children, a husband and a son to ageing parents. His wife was also working. He felt like he was juggling a gazillion balls. He had no idea what was crystal, rubber or concrete and he felt like he never had any time for himself. Kane was out of control and exhausted.

When I first started working with Kane, he didn't believe he had time to stop for coaching, so that was the first hurdle we had to overcome. I explained that lack of time was not an excuse. I challenged him to carve out five minutes of his day – taking himself away to the park, which was right outside his office, just to breathe deeply was his first step. Deep breathing stimulates the parasympathetic nervous system, which is responsible for the body's rest and relaxation response. It helps reduce the body's fight-or-flight response, promoting relaxation. It works!

Kane mastered the five minute park pause. Then we extended the goal, to incorporate self-reflection as part of that time. He pushed his time out to ten minutes. He also took his notebook with him and wrote down what was going on for him. He then extended his time to 15 minutes and started labelling the balls he was juggling every day. In that time, he also reflected on the root causes of his overwhelm and his 'bad' busyness.

Kane realised he was a people pleaser. He was trying to keep everyone happy, and that was what was driving his decision-making. Rather than making conscious and better decisions for himself about what he said yes to, he automatically said yes to everything. Even when he knew it was a poor decision! He wasn't delegating enough, and he wasn't asking for help. He took on way too much beyond his capacity. By understanding this, he then had the choice of whether he made a change – and he did.

Kane came to recognise the power of pausing: how it increased his self-awareness and helped him gain control of his life. He understood which balls he could let bounce and which were concrete. He was able to say no to the right things. Kane felt like he was back in the driver's seat of his life. This concept changed his life, and it resurrected his career. On the rare day that he didn't do this practice – and that happens – he felt the difference in his stress levels. When he didn't do it, he felt out of control; when he did it, he felt like he was in control and more resilient. That is the power of doing this practice.

You might think that this won't work for you. Imagine how you would feel if it could. What would be different for you? Try it for a day and then for a week. It might make you feel uncomfortable, or you might think that you'll ruminate too much. We often need to feel the discomfort to entice us to move out of it. If you feel uncomfortable, that's often where your growth is, and that's exciting.

UNMASKING UNDERLYING PATTERNS

This is where the power of self-reflection kicks in and we take it to another level. When you make time for self-reflection you can identify negative habits and patterns that lead to overwhelm – for example, being a people pleaser, or even a control freak. I'm going to share with you eight different types of busy that become habits and contribute to overwhelm. Understanding which habits are running your life will give you the power of choice.

All of these types of busy contribute to your overwhelm in various ways. They are not clinical terms; this is a lighthearted way to assess how you 'do' busy. The aim is to become more aware of common patterns of behaviour that lead to juggling an unreasonable number of balls and, eventually, overwhelm. I cover these in more detail in my workshops and keynotes. Here is a summary:

1. *The badge of honour wearer*: Busyness becomes a badge of honour that you wear loudly and proudly. You feel a high level of importance wearing this badge and you talk about it constantly. You waste a lot of time by doing this.

2. *The control freak:* You believe you must maintain control over situations, tasks, people and events. You don't have the trust or belief that anyone else can do anything as well as you. You like things your way. You're often a micromanager or a perfectionist. You're reluctant to ask for help because that would mean you're not coping (in your mind).

3. *The people pleaser:* People pleasing is a common cause of overwhelm. It's where your focus is on pleasing others rather than yourself. Saying no to others causes extreme guilt, often stemming from the need to be liked and to avoid conflict. You need the approval of others and fear rejection. You're reluctant to ask for help because you like to see yourself as the helper.

4. *The disorganised jumble:* You are often flying by the seat of your pants. You're totally reactive and you often feel out of

control. You might realise you have a meeting ten minutes after the meeting has started. You're often late or miss deadlines. Or you'll constantly work all hours of the night to meet a deadline. You might look dishevelled. You like to think you're spontaneous but really, you're unconsidered.

5. *The FOMO fanatic*: FOMO is the fear of missing out. You often attend events or meetings just so you don't miss out on anything. You have an insatiable need to know what is going on around you. You'll butt into conversations, eavesdrop and be tethered to your phone. After all, you can't possibly miss out on anything that's happening in the social media landscape! You hate being out of the loop.

6. *The snapper*: You are angry because you are busy. Your aggressiveness and demeanour can push people away and make them feel like they want to avoid you at all costs. You snap and get defensive at the offer of help, saying you can do things yourself rather than allowing others to assist. The snapper often goes hand in hand with the control freak.

7. *The comfort zoner*: You love to do only what you know. You will do familiar, often menial, tasks rather than learning something new or trying a new way of doing things. You're a procrastinator. You are the one who prefers to answer emails rather than working on the most critical task on your to-do list. You put off things that feel hard.

8. *The drama queen*: You make your busyness known in the most dramatic way. You might sigh loudly, slam the desk or complain to whoever will listen. Often there are public tears because you're so busy and everyone will know about it. You thrive on the attention you get from being so dramatic.

When I present this information to audiences, I find that people will resonate with at least two of the types of busy. You might have read through the list thinking, 'Yep, that's me. I identify with all of those.' We can cycle through all the types depending on our situation and capacity. I am often a blend of control freak and drama queen. I can get very dramatic when I become overwhelmed due to being a control freak and not asking for help! My husband will tell you I become quite vocal around the fact that I'm just so busy. It's a pattern I can repeat now and again, but I'm getting better at circumventing it.

The power is in understanding what type of busy you are doing most of the time. It's not about finding out what you're doing 'wrong' so you can beat yourself up and feel bad about it. It's about being more self-aware of your own behaviour so you can make conscious changes if need be.

Identifying your type isn't difficult to do; often, it's the simple things that make the biggest difference. It's like looking at a cake recipe to understand what you need to include so you can make a delicious fluffy cake that rises and tastes good. You also need to understand what you *don't* want to include. Perhaps simply using self-raising flour rather than plain flour will achieve your result.

The patterns that cause your overwhelm aren't limited to what I have shared here. Let these serve as a thought starter for you. You know yourself best.

You can't solve or avoid your overwhelm if you're not aware of the root cause. Going back to Kane's story, he identified as a people pleaser and that was the reason he was juggling a lot of concrete balls. Once he identified that, he could drop those balls for good. He only realised that he was a people pleaser because he pressed the pause button.

You might say, 'I already know the reason that I'm busy. I don't need to do this exercise.' If you already know the reason, you have a choice whether you continue with your strategy or not. You've picked up this book for a reason.

During your reflection time, think about what is not working. What type of busy are you? What are you constantly reacting to? Are you not delegating tasks? Are you not asking for help? Are you not making time for yourself? Are you not exercising? These are just some examples of what might not be working. Write everything down. Ask yourself empowering questions; for example:

- What prevents me from delegating?
- What prevents me from making time for myself?
- What's the cause of my people pleasing?

It's important that you don't ask yourself 'why' questions. These mostly limit your thinking to a justification that disempowers you. Allow the justifications to flow if they are there – and they will be – but explore beyond them. This is what will make the difference. What is the deeper reason for the decisions that you are making?

For example, I recognised I was a control freak when I took on one of my largest leadership roles. Upon starting the role, I was doing far too many tasks that could have been delegated. I believed that I could 'do it all' and that I would do it best. I also believed it would take far too long to explain what I needed done to one of my team members.

As a result I rapidly spun out of control and became overwhelmed. I would dread going to work on a Monday wondering what else would be added to my ginormous workload. I started asking myself why I was so busy and why this was so hard. I could certainly find all the reasons why, but it wasn't helping me – it was only compounding the problem.

I eventually carved out some time on a Friday afternoon after thinking that there must be a better way. And there was! Carving out that time, disruption free, gave me the space to think and reflect on what was going wrong for me. I asked myself, how can I do this better? What do I need to stop doing to turn this around? What can I start doing that will help me? The lightbulbs went on!

I put my hand up and asked for help. And what do you know, other people knew how to help me and help me well! It took me a while to dig myself out of my self-dug hole and change my way of working, but I did it. I created a new working rhythm that worked for me and empowered others.

What I didn't realise was that by being a control freak, I made others feel I didn't trust them. This was the last thing I was trying to do. My role became enjoyable and I felt like I was back in the game. The pausing practice for me became a ritual. This is the exact moment it started for me.

It can work for you, too.

You might be wondering how the pause works in a crisis situation. If you have built up the practice of pausing, this will help you in a crisis – because the last thing you want to do in a crisis is react when you need to be taking considered action. Pausing allows you a moment to self-regulate and consider your response. When life events happen – and they often do, on different scales – you'll need to adapt. By taking the time to pause, you'll be able to adapt quicker.

CONCLUSION

In this chapter, you've learned about the power of the pause. You now have a strategy for how to press pause. You know that pressing pause expands your self-awareness and provides you with the opportunity to self-regulate, respond and adapt to any situation. You know it can help you uncover the underlying patterns that are causing your overwhelm. I'm delighted for you because I know from personal experience how powerful this strategy is. It is necessary to build your resilience and lead a life you love. It is life changing.

Stop going through life accepting things as they are. Start pushing the pause button daily and make it a habit. By doing this, you will discover the immense benefit to your life – just like Kane did.

You now know the foundational steps to avoiding overwhelm and increasing self-awareness. In the next chapter, I'm going to show you how to reclaim your life and take charge by living and leading above the line. This is taking everything that we've discussed to another level and it's something you'll be able to implement across all areas of your life.

Chapter 3

THE POWER OF CHOICE

This chapter introduces you to one of the most impactful business models I learned about during my corporate career. It's called above the line and below the line. It represents choice. By mastering the art of choice, you become the empowered leader of your life. You'll be shaping your destiny through choice and conscious decision-making, taking ownership of your actions and embracing the mindset of responsibility for leading a life you love.

To master the art of choice, you need to develop a mindset of thoughtful decision-making and take responsibility for the consequences of your actions. This means making choices that align with your values, aspirations, long-term goals and priorities. It's being proactive in shaping your own path, rather than being passively influenced by external circumstances or succumbing to a victim mentality.

I'm not talking about the need to be perfect. Perfection is not on the agenda. It's about embracing imperfections, mistakes and failures as learning experiences and focusing on progress instead.

Acknowledging emotions such as anger, disappointment, grief and frustration is important. It's okay to have an adult tantrum in private if you need to. The key distinction is how long you stay in that state of frustration and disappointment, or a 'poor me' moment, before you decide to move back above the line. It's about taking deliberate action to lead your life.

By taking ownership of your choices and recognising the importance of conscious decision-making, you will adapt quicker to change and build resilience. You'll be able to make the most of any situation that is thrown at you.

I was very angry when I was diagnosed with cancer. I wanted to blame someone or something for my situation, and I had someone to blame: the person who misdiagnosed me and who I felt destroyed my life. The melanoma on my foot was initially diagnosed as a wart and treated accordingly, making the melanoma worse. So many thoughts and feelings ran through my head, to the point that I had planned a course of legal action that I was going to take once I had recovered.

My surgeon, who operated on me to remove my cancer, visited me every day while I was in hospital to check on me and see how I was doing. I was going to ask him for his advice on what to do and how I could take action against this person when something clicked in my brain. Seeking revenge and playing the victim card was in total conflict to who I was as a leader. I realised I was operating well and truly below the line and that would not help me. My situation couldn't be reversed, even if that person took full responsibility for misdiagnosing me.

I found myself at a crossroads facing a pivotal moment. It was a juncture where I could have easily succumbed to bitterness and justified my grievances, but I chose to take ownership of my life and lead above the line. At that moment, everything shifted. My entire demeanour transformed and my outlook changed. I realised that, amid all the chaos that was going on in my head, I had the power to choose my response. I consciously chose to move back above the line, to dig into my resilience and direct all my energy towards my recovery.

This choice became a catalyst, propelling me forward on a path of growth and self-discovery. It gifted me invaluable life lessons. If I had not been open to see the lessons, they would have slipped through my fingers unnoticed. Among these lessons, one stood out in its significance: the power of choice. I held the key to shape my narrative. Every decision, every step I took towards healing, became an active defiance against negativity. I decided my cancer would not define me and I would live a life of purpose despite it.

> IN RETROSPECT, MY DIAGNOSIS WAS NOT ONLY A SETBACK BUT AN OPPORTUNITY IN DISGUISE.

It allowed me to tap into my inner strength, resilience and determination. It taught me that life's intricate tune to which we dance can change at any moment. We always have a choice to embrace hardship as a catalyst for growth or to surrender to its weight.

This is my favourite chapter of this book. It holds the key to success in all areas of your life. In this chapter, I'll be introducing the concept of being the leader of your life: how to understand your decision-making and the impact it has on your life. This chapter will revolutionise the way you perceive yourself, your choices and the immense power they hold. Get ready to rewrite the story of your life from this moment and become the true architect of your own destiny.

YOU ALWAYS HAVE A CHOICE

Certain life circumstances – such as losing a partner or the diagnosis of an illness – can make you feel as though your choices are limited or taken away. It's important to acknowledge this. However, amid such circumstances, there are still choices within your reach. Stephen Covey, author of *The 7 Habits of Highly Effective People*, said, 'While we can't always choose what happened to us, we can choose our response.' This is a quote I live by.

Conscious choice means making choices while being fully aware and deliberate about the factors involved. This includes the pros and cons of the decision. When presented with a problem or change, we often make conscious choices. (We also make choices unconsciously, based on habits, biases and beliefs. I will share more about this in chapter 5.) Making conscious decisions means considering the options and choosing what aligns with our values, goals and desired outcomes.

As I mentioned before, it's not about doing this perfectly every time a decision needs to be made. Life rarely allows you the luxury of time in decision-making. However, taking ownership of whatever choice you make is important. This means being responsible for your actions and non-actions, decisions and non-decisions and how these impact your life.

Action refers to actively engaging in a behaviour or taking deliberate steps to achieve a desired outcome. It involves starting and carrying out specific steps or behaviours in pursuit of a goal that you're trying to achieve or in response to a situation.

Non-action refers to refraining from taking action or choosing not to engage in a particular behaviour. It involves a conscious decision to withhold action or refrain from doing something. A common example of this is when people decide they are going to exercise. The decision is made to get up at 5.30am and hit the gym. When the alarm goes off, the snooze button is pressed, again, and again, and again – until it gets to the stage that it's too late to go to gym and the opportunity is missed. This is a non-action that has a consequence for the person's health.

Non-decision, also known as indecision or decision paralysis, refers to the state of being unable or unwilling to make a definitive choice or take decisive action. Non-decision arises from various factors such as fear of making the wrong choice, lack of information or clarity, conflicting priorities or a general difficulty in making decisions. Sometimes it's just all too hard! My friend Debbie is very intelligent but struggles to make a decision. She is very aware of this, but it doesn't seem to make a difference. She procrastinates to the point that she has missed out on putting herself forward for job opportunities, then is regretful of her non-decision, which has held her back in her career.

Identifying your actions, non-actions, decisions and non-decisions allows you to make empowered choices quicker and easier by understanding how these will impact your life. You'll end up being able to juggle the right number of balls for you. Even more importantly, you'll be juggling the right balls at any given time.

Soon after my surgery, I had to make a decision about my preventative treatment. I considered myself a newcomer to the medical arena. For most of my life, I had been very healthy. So, this was all very new to me. Treatment for melanoma is relatively new. If I had been diagnosed with stage three melanoma ten years ago, my chances of survival would have been slim. Thankfully, due to the incredible medical researchers, my chances had greatly improved.

It came down to three options:

1. Do nothing and choose not to have treatment.
2. Undergo immunotherapy treatment.
3. Undergo targeted tablet therapy.

I felt option one wasn't for me, as my cancer was aggressive and time was of the essence. My oncologist and surgeon explained the differences between options two and three. They provided me with handouts that detailed the two types of drugs used in immunotherapy and how they were administered. They detailed side effects that were pages long. I was told option three, the targeted tablet therapy, would make me feel constantly ill, and I knew I didn't want that. The medical recommendation was to go with immunotherapy, which is unique in treating melanoma. To give you a bit of insight into what it is, usually, your immune system fights 'foreign' cells that cause illnesses and disease. However, cancer cells stop your immune system from destroying them and then spread through your body. Immunotherapy works by effectively switching on your body's immune system to fight cancer. This is the best-case scenario, of course. It's incredible what science can do!

Despite the recommendations, I was struggling to decide. It all felt too hard and too overwhelming. I had just had major surgery and my body hadn't healed yet. I was worried about whether it could cope with the brutality of such a treatment. I also had a fear of needles, and immunotherapy is administered intravenously. The fact was I didn't want to have to choose a treatment at all – I wanted to stay in my little cocoon of home, live in a bubble of denial and magically get better. However, that was not my reality, and I had to decide.

So, I pressed pause, moved myself back above the line and consciously considered my options. I reconnected with who I want to be as a leader. I decided I would have immunotherapy and I would lead myself according to one of my top values: courage. This was a time I needed to step up and lead, and practise what I preach! I share how you can do this too in the remaining chapters.

You might think, 'I don't have a choice for many of the things I have to do in my life. I don't choose for my child to love football, which means I have to run around and take them to training three nights a week and games that take up my entire weekend.' Ultimately, you *do* have a choice. You make the choice to take your child to training. As hard or begrudging as those choices might be, you're making or have made them, and there was a driving force behind those decisions.

Take a moment to reflect on the balls you're juggling right now. Do any of them make you feel miserable? Are you juggling them begrudgingly? Write these balls down then think about the choices you are making in juggling them. Is the ball aligned to your priorities? (We'll talk more about that in chapter 6.)

You might feel as though you don't have the option to make any other choice. In this case, try to imagine what you *would* do if you had a choice. You'll be surprised what might shift if you can imagine a different result or change how you think about that ball – similar to how I reimagined the 'treatment ball' I was juggling. Give it a go. Let your mind run with it and see where it takes you.

YOU ARE THE LEADER OF YOU

To become an effective leader of others, it is essential to first lead yourself. Your ability to guide and inspire those around you is limited without self-leadership. By recognising and embracing your role as the leader of you and your life, you lay the foundation for a fulfilling and impactful existence. Leadership extends beyond the confines of your organisation or where you work. It permeates every aspect of your life. As a parent, you play one of the most significant leadership roles of all, guiding and shaping the lives of your children. You might be a teacher, a caregiver, an aunt, an uncle, a sibling or a leader in your community – you are a leader.

In 2010, well-known educator and author Peter Drucker said that self-leadership is to serve as chief, captain or CEO of one's own life. I love this definition and it's a great way to think about it. You have the ability to influence how you think, feel, act and lead yourself towards the life that you love. That's powerful.

> BEING A LEADER OF YOU IS THE VERY DEFINITION OF LEADING ABOVE THE LINE. IT'S TAKING RESPONSIBILITY AND ACCOUNTABILITY FOR EVERY PART OF YOUR LIFE.

You're responsible for leading:
- your happiness
- your health
- your wealth
- your career
- your relationships

- your spirit
- your growth
- your life.

It's not up to others to make you happy, wealthy or wise. You need to do that for you first. That's within your control.

It is also within your control to consciously choose how you lead and the impact that you have on others' lives. Everyone has a sphere of influence. By leading by example and in line with the person you want to be, you inspire those within your sphere to see what is possible for them. Through acts of kindness and encouragement, you can ignite the potential in others and create the ripple effect of positive change. The way you lead your own life serves as a blueprint for others to follow, showcasing the possibility for their life. Embracing the mindset of a leader not only empowers those around you, but cultivates your own resilience and adaptability.

McKinsey & Co has conducted research about the skills we'll need to thrive in the future world of work. Interestingly, self-leadership is one of the four critical skills. The organisation has looked at the kinds of jobs that will be lost, as well as those that will be created as AI and robotics take hold. The research identified 56 deltas, which are a mix of skills and attitudes across 13 skill groups in four categories. Digital fluency is, of course, what we all need now and moving forward with the advance of technology. But self-leadership is also one of the four categories most important to the future of work. Self-leadership includes self-awareness and self-management, courage and risk-taking and ownership and decisiveness – all of which I cover in this book. But not only is self-leadership important for the future of work and your career but also the success of your personal life. By developing this skill, you are ensuring your future resilience.

Sometimes the concept of being a leader regardless of title can be foreign and difficult to get your head around. Some have said to me, 'I've never thought of myself this way before.' We all have areas of weakness and strength in this area. You might be great at leading yourself at work, but not so great at home or with your health. If you are leading all areas of your life, I applaud you. If not, this could serve as a timely reminder. You might also fall off the wagon from time to time, like I do.

Start thinking about yourself as the leader of you. We'll look at this in more detail in chapters 6 and 7, but you can ask yourself these questions now:

- Are my choices and actions reflective of the leader I want to be?
- Am I someone who takes responsibility for my actions or do I have a tendency to point my finger at someone else?

Remember, there is no judgement here. This is a self-awareness exercise. The more honest you can be, the better your outcome.

It's common to think, 'I don't want to be a leader at work. My boss plays that role. There is no way I can be a leader.' Some people fear the responsibility of being a leader, but embracing it at the level I'm suggesting will help you create a life that you love, both professionally and personally. I'm not asking you to do anything overtly – just try thinking of yourself as a leader for a week and notice the difference it makes for you.

LEADING ABOVE THE LINE

It's always helpful to have a point of reference to show us how we are leading. I've been referring to being above or below the line throughout this book in relation to choice. This is the most outstanding model that I learned during my corporate career and adapted across all areas of my life. It encourages us to start consciously thinking about the choices and decisions we are making. According to Carl Jung, who is regarded as one of the most influential psychologists in history, 'Until you make the unconscious conscious, it will direct your life and you will call it fate.'

The model won't change your fate, but it will help you make choices and take control.

It's simple to enact. You just have to think, am I leading in a way that is above or below the line right now? Perhaps think of it like 'location, location, location', which is a term real estate agents use when spruiking a property in a prime location. It's the easy way to self-check your location; whether you're above or below the line.

We choose which side of the line we sit on. If it sounds simple, that's because it is. But in its simplicity lies its strength. I've adopted this model to highlight the power of choice. I often call it the victim or victor model (see figure 2).

At a high level, operating above the line is being open and positive. It's about responsibility, accountability and owning your choices. Operating below the line is where you are closed. It's where you operate in a negative space. It's about denial, excuses, defensiveness and blame.

If you refer to the model overleaf, you'll see that I have 'conscious' at the top and 'unconscious' down the bottom. When you are operating above the line, you are making a conscious or deliberate choice about your leadership. You are making a deliberate choice on how to react to any situation thrown at you. You're solution-focused, resilient, curious, open to learning, and taking ownership and responsibility for your choices. You're open to listening to others' opinions and ideas and want to learn about new things and expand your mind. You're inclusive and empathetic. You're also accountable for your choices. This is the definition of being a victor. You are winning at life.

Figure 2: Leading above or below the line

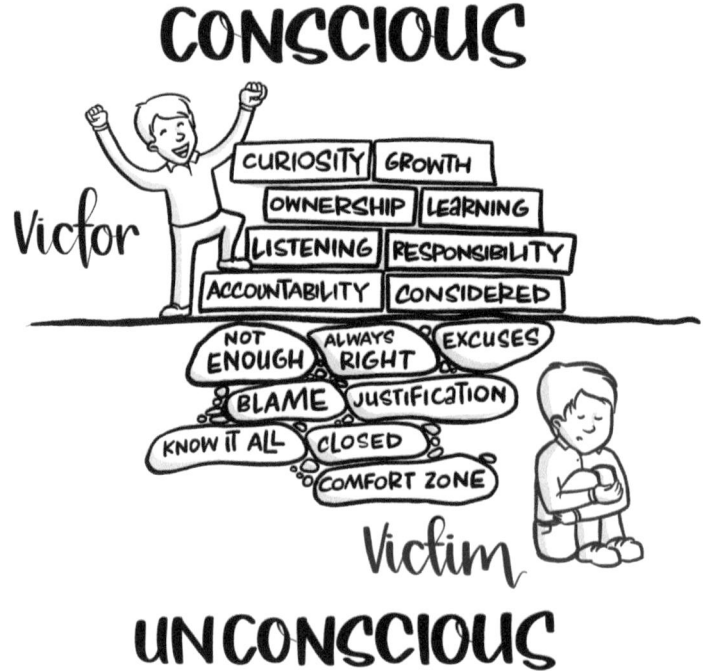

Operating above the line is not about being unreasonably positive or optimistic. It's not about forbidding yourself from feeling disappointment, frustration, grief, sadness or anger. The distinction is, when you're operating above the line you'll be curious about *why* you're feeling how you feel. You'll be curious about the change that's happening or the decision that you made. Living above the line is about being open to learning what you can from any situation, challenge or obstacle, rather than being victim to it.

Below that line is where you fall victim to your circumstances. It's where people often think they know it all. They're not open to other people's points of view. They look at things as glass-half-empty rather than glass-half-full. Nothing is enough. They may believe that they're not good enough or don't have the skills to achieve the success that they want to achieve. Operating below the line means that they're closed to learning. They stay within their comfort zone. They're not willing to step out of it and learn new things.

When you're below the line, you often have the need to be right and will try to win an argument at all costs. You want to blame others for your situation. You want to point the finger. Everything needs to be someone else's fault. You constantly try to justify what you may have done wrong with an excuse like 'I'm too busy' or 'I don't have time', rather than taking ownership or responsibility for the error. You're basically full of excuses.

An important thing to understand is that, as humans, we are hardwired to operate below the line. Our brain is programmed to perceive threats. When the brain detects danger, it triggers the activation of the sympathetic nervous system, commonly known as the fight-or-flight response. This response involves the release of cortisol, a hormone that raises blood sugar levels and suppresses the immune system. It allows the body to allocate energy towards addressing the perceived threat. This allows humans and other mammals to survive when they perceive a genuine threat. The issue for us in the modern day is that our brains can't tell the difference between a threat to our survival and a threat to our ego or identity. We can often react or get defensive out of habit. When we do that, we fall into a victim state, which is below the line.

> **IF YOU FIND YOURSELF BELOW THE LINE, UNDERSTAND THAT IT'S OFTEN INSTINCTUAL. THE POSITIVE THING IS THAT YOU HAVE A CHOICE WHETHER YOU STAY THERE OR NOT.**

The line is a powerful self-reflection tool that you can use to reflect on situations retrospectively, too. It will help you understand your location around choices you've made in the past: whether you were acting instinctively or through habit and reverting below the line; or whether you were operating above the line and taking full responsibility and accountability for your situation, decision or choice. Ultimately, understanding the difference between operating above or below the line empowers you to take control of your life.

I used this tool when I was looking to blame the person who misdiagnosed me. The fact was, I was looking for revenge. I was way below the line. I was choosing to be a victim, and I wanted to point the finger at someone. I wanted to blame that person for my situation. I had made an unconscious decision to do that. It was an instinct because the misdiagnosis threatened my life, and I was so angry. But then, I asked myself if I wanted to live above or below the line, and I could see I had a choice. I decided to live above the line. I took responsibility for my situation. I dug into my resilience. That's when everything changed for me.

You might be thinking, 'I can't be above the line all the time.' And you're right. You won't always be above the line. We all dip below the line at times. What matters is how long you choose to stay there. I'm definitely not suggesting that you need to be positive or happy all the time, either. I believe that's impossible and inauthentic. You don't need to be someone who is flawless and takes responsibility for everything. For example, you will often feel frustrated when you are above the line. But the difference is, you'll be curious as to why you're feeling that way, and you will take responsibility for how you're feeling and not take it out on others.

Try this. Reflect on a situation when you have experienced frustration. You might have been sitting in traffic, or maybe you wanted to make a quick dash into the supermarket and faced a huge queue. Write about what frustrated you about the situation. For example, did you feel inconvenienced? I use these two examples because they are my bugbears when I believe I am 'busy' and my dramatic tendencies come out! I huff and puff and become very frustrated. Not how I want to be. Think about your reaction. In what ways were your thoughts and behaviours above the line or below the line? Write them down. How can you react differently when that happens?

Leaders often ask me, 'Why do I always have to be the bigger person?' The question particularly arises when their team members aren't taking responsibility or accountability for their role or behaviour. A similar challenge is when your children may not be doing what is expected, and you think, 'Why is it always up to me?' This is the true test of a leader – and remember, you are one. It can be challenging to be the bigger person, but ultimately that's what true leadership is about. Understand that no matter what, you have a choice about which side of the line you operate on – always.

CONCLUSION

In this chapter, you have learned that you always have a choice in how you respond to any situation that is thrown your way. You have also learned that you are the leader of your life, and the importance of the word 'leader' in that phrase. We are all leaders and role models, regardless of title. When we embrace a leadership mindset and understand we all have a choice in how we lead our life, it's a game-changer. I'm delighted to have shared this with you as something new or as a reminder. It's a simple but powerful strategy that is easy to refer to.

Stop thinking that life just happens to you or that you don't have a choice in life and you need to accept things for how they are. Start leading your life and understand you have the power of choice to lead yourself and your life in a direction that you will love.

In the next chapter, I will show you how you can embrace change, big or small. I will explain the difference between accepting, resisting and resigning to change, and how it can propel you forward, build your resilience and help you tap into strength that you might not have known that you have.

Chapter 4

EMBRACING CHANGE, BIG OR SMALL

One Friday night in 2010, I was having drinks at home with a friend when a freak storm hit. It was intense – one of those storms where you hide inside, waiting for it to pass. Water began coming through the ceiling and down the wall, which is never good. I got a bucket, placed it under the drips, and got some towels to mop up the water. Once the storm subsided, we went outside to survey the damage. I lived inner city, so there wasn't much to look for other than street flooding.

I thought I'd escaped pretty lightly, given the intensity of the storm. I called a roof plumber the following day, who came to look at the roof and sorted the problem so no further water could enter the ceiling if there were any more storms. I thought that was the end of the situation. It wasn't. I was in for some unexpected and unwelcome change.

Some months later, I noticed a problem with my floorboards in the kitchen. They appeared to be expanding and buckling. It was strange. I thought the recent rain was causing it, and it would soon return to normal. Then I noticed it happening in the lounge room as well and alarm bells rang. Unbeknown to me, during the storm, water had also gotten under the house and caused significant damage to my home. This became an insurance job.

> **CHANGE IS AN UNDENIABLE FORCE THAT SHAPES OUR LIVES. IT IS A CONSTANT COMPANION, WHETHER WE INVITE IT IN WILLINGLY OR IT BARGES IN UNINVITED, CAUSING RIPPLES OF UNEASE.**

Change doesn't have to be monumental to leave a big impact on our lives. It can manifest in the tiniest of shifts that suddenly alter the course of our journey.

Invited or welcome change occurs when you start the change yourself. You might decide to do a renovation or change jobs. Unwelcome change can include things such as the pandemic, a health diagnosis or workplace restructuring. These are all unwelcome changes that can be incredibly unsettling.

Even when we instigate change, though, it can unsettle us; we can experience the same response as we do for uninvited change. For example, think about deciding to move house. That's one of the most stressful situations you can enter into. There are ripple effects of unease that occur even when you've made a decision to change.

The ability to distinguish between the kinds of change and the state of mind you are in – whether that be acceptance, resistance or resignation – is the difference between embracing change or resenting it.

Initially, I eagerly embraced the three-month move to a serviced apartment while my own home was repaired, curious about the change it would bring. However, what was supposed to be a short period dragged on for nine long months, causing worry, financial strain and frustration. Dealing with difficult builders only added to my challenges. I was pushed well below the line. I started to feel like a victim. I couldn't manage to change the situation until I confided in a friend and discovered a way to work through the problems. Slowly, I shifted my mindset and became curious about how I could improve things. My perspective transformed from seeing the situation as a nightmare to an opportunity. I pondered what I could do to feel more in control. Choosing between acceptance, resistance and resignation helped me to manage myself through the hard times.

In this chapter, we'll explore the constant nature of change and its transformative power when embraced. I will delve into the three distinct responses that change evokes: acceptance, resistance and resignation. These responses hold the power to elevate you above the line or to drag you beneath it. I'll show you how accepting any change can benefit your life, regardless of its scale or circumstance, whether it's welcome or unwelcome.

CHANGE IS YOUR CERTAINTY

Change is constant. It manifests on various scales, from grand societal shifts to deeply personal transformations. Change is inevitable as we go through life. Embracing personal change can be challenging, requiring acceptance and adaptation. It compels us to engage in self-reflection, as discussed in chapter 2.

Just as a caterpillar undergoes a complete metamorphosis, change involves a process of growth, transition and transformation, leading to a new and beautiful state – if it is embraced and accepted.

Your perception of whether a change is positive or negative depends on your individual perspective, cultural values and the impact of the change on your life. These things will also influence your response to change. When the pandemic hit, many struggled with the forced and unwelcome change, while others relished it. The individual responses to it were very dependent on people's life and financial situations. Importantly, change need not be monumental to have a profound impact. It can be as intimate as losing a job, ending a relationship, facing a health diagnosis or encountering a major life transition such as parenthood or retirement.

Change often stirs unsettling emotions and disrupts our sense of order. Being diagnosed with melanoma cancer elicited an emotional reaction from me before I even considered the practical aspects. It turned my life upside down and was very unsettling. I have had several clients who have received redundancy packages. While one person may be ecstatic about it and looking forward to a break or a new career, another will be upset, fearful and worried about what's next. Responses to change vary, as each person's experience of it is unique.

As we navigate a lifetime of change, adaptability and resilience become key. Embracing change can be transformational, reshaping our beliefs and behaviours, regardless of its scale. It encourages us to self-reflect, challenge our assumptions and limitations and learn new things. During the pandemic, many were forced to embrace new-to-them technology to maintain relationships with family, friends and teammates. My parents had never used video to communicate, but found themselves having to learn Zoom to celebrate birthdays and other special occasions.

Faced with change, it is vital to remain flexible with our personal and professional goals. Change affects us in diverse ways, causing adjustments to our strategies and actions. No longer can we set goals and forget them; rather, we must continuously align them to incorporate the inevitable changes that will occur.

While pain and uncertainty may accompany change, looking for its potential upsides can ease our pain and allow us to embrace the change.

> OVER TIME, A SHIFT IN PERSPECTIVE ALLOWS US TO SEE THE SILVER LININGS EVEN AMID CHALLENGING CHANGES.

Having encountered numerous changes throughout my life, I know this to be true: you are stronger than you think and you can dig deeper into your resilience than you ever thought possible when you embrace change. It is a catalyst for growth and learning.

In her book *Becoming*, former First Lady Michelle Obama shares her personal journey of transformation. Throughout the book, she eloquently recounts her experiences and the pivotal moments that shaped her into the woman she became. One specific story that stood out to me was about her transition from high-powered corporate lawyer to becoming the First Lady of the United States. In the book she reflects on her initial resistance to the idea of her husband Barack running for presidency. She expresses her concerns about the toll this change would take on their family life and the immense pressure they would face. However, as she witnessed the growing movement and the impact her husband's message was having on people, she recognised the significance of the opportunity for change.

Michelle Obama writes about her internal struggle and how she ultimately found the strength to embrace the transformative power of change. She shares her realisation that their lives had been leading to this moment. She chose to embrace the challenge and the uncertainty that lay ahead.

Throughout the story, she also illustrates the complexities of change. She highlights the importance of examining your own fears and doubts – and ultimately finding the courage to step outside your comfort zone in pursuit of a greater purpose. The story serves as an inspiring example of how change, even when doubting, can lead to personal and societal transformation.

Michelle Obama ultimately moved from being below the line – where she was resisting the change and angry at her husband for taking on roles that impacted her family's personal lives – to above the line – where she embraced the change, found her voice and stepped into a new role. She became a role model for many, particularly women, as the first African-American woman to hold the position of First Lady. Her experiences left a powerful legacy and she continues to inspire others to embrace change and strive for a better future.

You might think it's impossible for you to accept change and see it as something positive because the change you're facing is an injustice. You might consider accepting unjust change as the definition of toxic positivity. Change is often unwarranted, unjustified and even completely unfair. But if you don't accept it for what it is, you'll never be able to have hope or navigate your way through it. You'll stay stuck in a victim mindset and, from experience, I can tell you that absolutely sucks.

When you move from a victim mindset to a solution-focused approach you can examine the change with curiosity. What can you learn from it? You can still feel sadness, anger, grief or whatever emotions you feel about it; but just believing that you can change your state, even for a minute, can support you to find a solution to navigate the change. If you are feeling depressed and stuck after trying the strategies that I'm sharing, try talking it through with a friend like I did when I was feeling like a victim of my circumstances with my house. If that doesn't help, you can seek professional advice about the change you are experiencing. You might benefit from more one-on-one help.

Take some time to reflect on a change you have experienced, or a period of stability in your life that ended. It might have been a job loss or a relationship breakup, for example. Consider your response to it. Do you think you accepted, resisted or resigned yourself to the change? How did that make you feel? Did you learn something from the situation or dismiss it as a negative experience? For example, if you lost your job, did you decide to never work in that industry again or did you get a better-paying job at a higher level? Knowing what you do now, could you have responded to the situation differently to achieve a better outcome?

You don't have to feel great about the change. Just accept it and see what you can do to move yourself back above the line. It will help you feel better. Give it a go.

CHOOSING EMPOWERMENT OVER DEFEAT

Our decision to accept, resist or resign to change influences our outcome. Understanding the transformative potential of acceptance is key to growth and resilience. When we resist change, which is common, we create barriers that impede our progress and growth. Resistance to change often leads to feelings of frustration, anxiety and defeat. Instead of embracing change and new possibilities, we cling to familiar routines and comfort zones, preventing us from exploring the potential benefits that change can offer. This can keep us tethered to the past, meaning we stagnate. When we actively acknowledge and adapt to change, we embrace acceptance, taking charge of our responses. Resignation is a passive surrender, accepting circumstances without attempting to change. However unwelcome the change may be, accepting it opens the door to taking action.

You might have come across the popular saying, 'It is what it is.' This expression captures the essence of facing frustrating or challenging situations that seem beyond our control but demand acceptance. Its origins trace back to a 1949 article by JE Lawrence in the *Nebraska State Journal* which detailed the harsh and unyielding nature of frontier-era life in Nebraska. 'New land is harsh and vigorous and sturdy. It scorns evidence of weakness. There is nothing of sham or hypocrisy in it. It is what it is, without apology.'

Often, change just is what it is!

Acceptance

Acceptance ignites hope and possibility. We all need hope. Hope reduces feelings of helplessness and helps us to look for a brighter future.

I absolutely love daffodils. They sprout during winter as a sign of hope for warmer days ahead in spring. The daffodil has become a symbol of hope for cancer organisations worldwide, representing support for all those affected by cancer. The association with spring and new beginnings is fitting, signifying the promise of renewal and growth. Renowned author and motivational speaker Zig Ziglar said, 'If there is hope in the future, there is literally power in the present.' I believe that is what acceptance grants us: the power to move forward. Acceptance allows us to acknowledge the reality of our circumstances and let go of resistance or denial. By accepting the changes that come our way, we free ourselves from the burden of fighting against the inevitable. In the state of acceptance, we become receptive to new opportunities and perspectives. We open ourselves up to the potential for positive outcomes, even in the face of uncertainty. Acceptance enables us to see beyond the limitations imposed by change and to explore alternative paths. It empowers us to learn to adapt and discover hidden strengths within ourselves. It also enables us to move above the line.

Personality can influence how change affects our wellbeing. Major life changes can cause stress for people who feel more comfortable in a routine or who seek certainty in life.

One well-known fictional character who often found comfort in his routine and sought certainty in life was the beloved cartoon cat Garfield, created by Jim Davis. We know him for his love of lasagna, disdain for Mondays and desire for a life of ease and predictability. He seeks the comfort of his favourite spots, like his cosy bed or the windowsill, and shows reluctance towards any disruptions to his routine. While Garfield's disinclination to step outside his comfort zone leads to humour, it also reminds us of the human desire for stability.

Change is often more easily welcomed by those who seek novelty and spontaneity in their life. Madonna has a reputation for embracing change and spontaneity. Throughout her illustrious career as a singer, actor and entrepreneur, Madonna has consistently reinvented herself and her music. She has adopted various personas and styles, making her a true chameleon in the entertainment industry. From her early days as a provocative pop icon in the 1980s to her exploration of different music genres and artistic expressions in subsequent decades, Madonna's willingness to evolve and experiment has been a hallmark of her success.

Resistance

Resistance is an inherent part of change, often emerging as a natural response to the unfamiliar nature of transformation. When you face change, you may instinctively cling to what is familiar, resisting the need to adapt or let go of what is known. Resistance can manifest in various ways, such as denial, avoidance or even outright opposition. It stems from a sense of fear, uncertainty or a perceived threat to our stability or identity. I spoke about this in chapter 3, where I shared that we are hardwired to identify threats and often see change as a threat. So, it can be a natural response to initially resist change rather than welcoming it with open arms, until we have assessed the situation.

Throughout my corporate career, I faced regular, significant change. Whether it was a change in organisational structure, job role, manager or expectations – there was a lot of it. At first, I would resist any unwelcome change. I was fearful of what it would mean for me. I was comfortable and confident with the way things were and I wanted to retain the status quo. Of course, that made it worse for me at the time and I was lucky that I had people around me to support me and help me see the opportunity that the change represented. I eventually embraced it, but it certainly wasn't my first instinct for a number of years.

You may resist change because it challenges your established routines, requires you to acquire new skills or knowledge or forces you to confront an uncomfortable truth about yourself or the world around you.

> **WHILE RESISTANCE IS A NATURAL REACTION, IT CAN ALSO HINDER GROWTH.**

By stubbornly resisting change, you might find yourself trapped in the status quo, becoming irrelevant. Companies such as the iconic film and camera company Kodak and the video rental company Blockbuster are good examples. The people who led these companies refused to embrace the digital revolution to their detriment and extinction. The advancement of technology is something that people often resist. Not only can this make life much harder for them personally but they can make themselves professionally redundant, too.

When reflecting on change and becoming curious about it, your resistance can serve as a valuable source of insight. It highlights areas where you feel most vulnerable or are attached to the status quo. It can shed light on your deepest fears and insecurities. By acknowledging and exploring your resistance – in other words, by moving above the line – you gain the opportunity for self-reflection and growth. You can examine the underlying beliefs and assumptions that are holding you back, and open yourself up to new perspectives and possibilities.

Resignation

Resignation to change can be a default response, too, when we believe the change is hard or unwelcome. Resignation is often born from feelings of hopelessness, helplessness or disillusionment. It breeds a sense of defeat and a belief that making the best of a situation is futile. This feeling can reduce your problem-solving abilities. For instance, when facing job loss, someone who resigns themselves may feel defeated and convinced that finding new employment is impossible. They may stop searching for opportunities, settling for stagnation.

Resignation can also create a feeling of being trapped and stuck, a familiar sentiment many of my clients encounter in their careers. They resign themselves to the limitations of their organisation or leader, convinced that change can only come from within. Yet they hesitate to seek alternate options, choosing to resign themselves to the situation as it is, believing that change isn't possible.

This response to change often occurs unconsciously, becoming a default reaction to challenging circumstances.

Breaking free from resignation requires you to recognise that change is possible, and take proactive steps to explore new opportunities – even if those steps are very small. Once my clients have explored available job opportunities online or floated their CV with recruiters, the possibility for change opens up. Or they may choose to courageously use their voice and create the change they were looking for. Either way, it is only through action that they move from resignation to acceptance of their situation, and find hope.

My clients often acknowledge to me that while their circumstances may be challenging, they feel empowered to make a choice for their destiny – rather than leaving it in someone else's hands. By challenging the belief that change is impossible, you open the door to potential transformations and find the courage to create a brighter future.

THE POWER OF CHOICE

Understanding the differences between acceptance, resistance and resignation gives you the power of choice. It brings the distinctions into your conscious awareness, enabling you to choose your response.

> 66 IT DOESN'T MATTER WHAT HAPPENS TO YOU. WHAT MATTERS IS HOW YOU RESPOND – AND THIS IS WHAT YOU ALWAYS HAVE CONTROL OVER.

When I first received my diagnosis, a feeling of hopelessness washed over me. I believed I was at the mercy of the medical profession, facing an internal enemy intent on my demise. The confusing language from medical professionals increased my feeling of helplessness. They warned the cancer was aggressive and would return. They left me without hope. My mind was fixated on negative thoughts, viewing the cancer as an ominous threat. It was, that's true – but this mindset took me below the line where I was resigned to the situation rather than taking ownership of my choices.

In those difficult moments after my diagnosis, all I wanted was for someone to assure me, 'You're going to be okay.' But to this day, no medical professional has told me that. I felt defeated.

It was only as I accepted my situation, acknowledging the reality with an 'it is what it is' mentality, that I took my power back. I started on a fresh path, delving into research and seeking information about my condition. Empowerment surged within me. Armed with knowledge, I started questioning my treatment and the effects it had on me. 'Why am I on this medication? What is causing me to feel this way?' I demanded clarity, rejecting jargon and insisting on clear, comprehensive explanations. I sought stories of others who had faced melanoma and conquered it. I gave myself hope.

In doing so, I became my best advocate, guiding myself through a challenging situation I never wanted to face. Through acceptance and empowerment, I discovered inner strength I never knew existed. I took control of my journey, determined to carve a path to healing and wellbeing.

I can assure you, I still don't want to be in this situation. I don't want to have this threat of cancer hanging over my head. I don't want to still be receiving treatment. I don't think anyone in this situation does. However, I accept it and I make the best of my circumstances. I empower myself. I advocate for myself so that I have a sense of being in control of the uncontrollable. Once I started doing that, my experience changed.

> MY MINDSET SWITCHED FROM HOPELESSNESS TO GRATITUDE AND EMPOWERMENT.

Again, I'm not suggesting you ignore the challenging feelings that often arise when change occurs, such as frustration, grief or sadness. Give yourself the space to feel all the feelings; you want to process them, not suppress them. But don't allow yourself to become stuck in those feelings, or to believe that you can't feel differently. You can't operate above the line if you're in a victim mindset and feeling shitty about your situation. I felt this way at first, but then I became curious about it rather than resigning myself to it. This is not about suppressing feelings. It's about moving forward despite them.

If you are feeling depressed or highly anxious about a change in your situation or if it has impacted you financially, please seek professional help. Sometimes we can't be our own best coach or leader and that is completely okay. You can come back to this work another time.

Building on from the previous exercise, think again about that change you went through. Did you go into negative feelings first? How long did you stay there? If you identify that you're still in resignation around that change, ask yourself how you might see the situation differently. Can you approach it with curiosity and consider what you learned from the change? What do you think you can do differently when you next experience change?

ADAPTING AND OVERCOMING OBSTACLES

We often see an obstacle as a barrier, but there's a key distinction between the two – and this is significant when facing change. Scott Allen Curley talks about this in his book *Absolution: The Dark Path to Light*. From an early age, Scott experienced a roller-coaster of hardships, including abuse as a child, drug addiction, prison sentences and homelessness. Yet he used all these experiences as a vehicle for personal growth, turning his life around to become a self-made millionaire on a mission to inspire others. I had the privilege of interviewing Scott on my podcast *Leading You*. He explained to me that a barrier is something that is fixed, firm and cannot be knocked down or jumped over; whereas an obstacle is something that we can jump over, navigate around or move out of the way. If you see change as a barrier, this limits your belief that you can adapt. If you see it as an obstacle, you set your mind to finding out how you can get around it or even over it. The obstacle won't stop you from succeeding.

Obstacles can present in many shapes and sizes. Some common obstacles include a lack of clarity about the change, a lack of willingness to accept change, a fear of change and a negative mindset. Let's explore these.

A lack of clarity

When faced with change, it's common to feel uncertain or unclear about what the change entails or how it can affect your life when you don't understand it. A lack of clarity often leads to feeling overwhelmed. When you don't know what your options are or feel out of control, you can become stuck. If you recognise this lack of clarity around a change, you can use this awareness as a starting point to seek more information. You can move above the line quicker and actively engage in hunting down details, asking questions and exploring the potential impact of the change. Understanding your own tendency towards acceptance, resistance or resignation can motivate you to seek the clarity you need to make informed decisions and take action.

A lack of willingness

Sometimes the resistance to change arises from a lack of willingness to accept it. This might be because of your attachment to your comfort zone, fear of the unknown or your desire to maintain the status quo. Or it might simply feel like the change is in the too-hard basket! By understanding that acceptance can ignite hope and possibility, you can consciously adopt an optimistic mindset that is open and curious. This mindset allows you to explore the potential benefits and opportunities that change can bring, helping you overcome the initial resistance and embrace the change easier.

A fear of change

Fear is a powerful emotion that often accompanies change. It can manifest as fear of failure, fear of the unknown or fear of making a mistake. Understanding your response to change enables you to recognise fear as a natural part of the process. By acknowledging your fears and exploring them, you can address them more effectively.

You can develop strategies to manage fear such as seeking support from others, breaking down the change into smaller, manageable steps, or reframing your perspective to focus on potential growth and learning. This can all come from embracing change. I explore this further in chapter 7.

A negative mindset

As we explored in chapter 3, a negative mindset can be a significant obstacle to accepting change and embracing possibility. It can lead to pessimism, self-doubt and a sense of powerlessness. Self-awareness around your responses to change empowers you to recognise when you are slipping into a negative mindset and consciously choose to shift your perspective. By cultivating an optimistic mindset, focusing on the opportunities for growth and practising self-compassion, you can approach change with a more optimistic outlook.

By recognising and understanding acceptance, resistance and resignation, you can actively address the obstacles of lack of clarity, lack of willingness, fear of change and negative mindset. This understanding serves as a guide, helping you to navigate through these challenges and take meaningful steps towards leading a life you love, even amid the most chaotic change.

THE FOUR-STEP PROCESS

I have a four-step process that I'd like to share with you. I have used this process in my life, most recently with my diagnosis. It will help you adapt to change, overcome resistance and confidently navigate the situation to make it work for you.

1. Assess the change and what it means for you

Get clarity about the change. Make the time to sit down and think about it objectively. I like to think about change as if it were an olden-days black-and-white movie with no sound. This helps me to remove the emotion, which can often cloud my judgement.

Assess what the change means for you. What might the impact look like? Sometimes we can make situations seem a lot bigger than they actually are.

By carving out time for self-reflection, you can gain the clarity you need about the situation. You will also know if you need to gather more information to understand it better.

2. Assess the pros and cons

For this part of the exercise I suggest grabbing some paper and drawing a line down the middle so you have two columns. Then write 'pros' at the top of the left-hand column and 'cons' on the top of the right-hand column. Then make your list. By doing this, you take the information that is swirling around in your head, often causing you to feel out of control or overwhelmed, and put it into a format where you can objectively assess the change. Then you will know if you need to gather more information about the change to understand your course of action.

3. Identify your resistance, if any

Why are you resisting the change? Is it fear? Have you fallen below the line and into a negative mindset about it? Perhaps it's all too hard. Write this down. Where is the resistance coming from?

4. How can you reframe the situation to give you hope?

Assess the positives you listed in the 'pros' column earlier. How can these give you hope? How can they empower you? What can you learn, and how will the change allow you to step up and grow as a person?

By using this simple process, you will reframe change as an obstacle rather than a barrier, so you can navigate it with more confidence.

The day after my diagnosis, I was in a state of shock and had to make some tough calls to inform clients, friends and family members of my situation. Some tried to offer comfort, saying, 'You'll emerge from this experience a changed person. There's a gift in this.' But at that moment, I couldn't see it. How could they suggest there was a gift in something life-threatening? Their words triggered resentment, and I wanted to lash out in disbelief. I couldn't empathise with their well-intentioned encouragement; all I saw was an immense barrier and total lack of appreciation for the gravity of my situation.

For me, acceptance was not immediate. Resentment and resistance clouded my perspective, making it impossible for me to see how cancer could make me a better person. But as time passed and I accepted and embraced my situation, a shift occurred. I saw the gift I'd been given. Cancer became an opportunity, forcing me to pause and reflect on the life I was leading. It forced me to prioritise myself ahead of anyone else. It made me see how precious life and health is – because when it's taken away, it's all you wish for. I also assessed whether I was truly living a life I loved. The answer was a resounding 'no'.

With newfound clarity, I realigned my actions with my values, deciding what truly mattered to me and what I wouldn't compromise on. I also reframed the comments people shared with me, allowing myself to see that they believed in me and my ability to beat this. This further fuelled my resilience.

Identifying obstacles became crucial in my journey of change. Through using this four-step process, I not only made peace with my diagnosis but also embraced it as a catalyst for growth.

You might think, 'I can reframe for a while, but when I'm tired or sick, I feel defeated again.' In chapter 5 we will discuss how to reframe and overcome relapses, which are completely normal.

You might like to use the four-step process and apply it to a situation you are struggling with right now. See if it helps you see it differently and empowers you to move forward.

CONCLUSION

In this chapter, you have learned that change is inevitable and can be experienced on different scales. It could be a universal change that impacts you, or a personal change. Regardless of what the change is, it's how you respond to it that matters. You have learned the difference between accepting change, resisting it or resigning to it, and how to see resistance to change as an obstacle rather than a barrier. You're now empowered to make different choices.

I encourage you to approach change with a fresh perspective. Start seeing that you can acknowledge the pain, fear and uncertainty of change and still shift your perspective to approach it from above the line with a solution-focused mindset.

Now you know how to reframe change to help you adapt to it easier. In the next chapter, we will explore the impact of beliefs and attitudes on behaviour to break through comfort zones and change your outcomes. I'll show you some more tricks to harness your mindset as a guiding light that leads you towards a life that you love, both personally and professionally.

Chapter 5

YOUR MINDSET IS YOUR SUPERPOWER

We're incredibly fortunate in Australia to have one of the best healthcare systems in the world. I was placed into the care of the Peter MacCallum Cancer Centre, which is thought to have the best treatment for melanoma in Australia. This didn't change the fact that I was really scared. Up to this point in my life, I had avoided hospitals. I also had a huge fear of needles. I would do everything in my power to avoid having a blood test or immunisation. As a child, my mum would force us to have our flu jabs. I would hide in the bathroom and cling to the sink to avoid being detected. It didn't work! Then, at the doctor's surgery, I would hide behind a chair. You can imagine my anxiety when I found out I had to receive the Covid-19 vaccine.

As you can see, I had a lot of work to do on my mindset. After my initial panic and worry about what was to come, I called a friend who'd been through breast cancer. We shared a fear of needles. I asked her for advice. She explained how she reframed her fear of walking into the hospital to get her treatment to the state of being strong 'to fight the cancer bitch'. She felt empowered to do whatever it took to get her health back. She is now 11 years in remission. She changed her mindset from fear to empowerment.

I took her advice. I reframed my fear to one of strength. It didn't happen at the click of a finger; I did it progressively. This was an ingrained fear! I chose a new way to think about needles. I imagined them making me well, making me strong and getting me back to living a life cancer-free. This motivated and inspired me to move forward – to let go of my fear and to step into a positive mindset. I repeated the words 'strong and cancer-free' over and over again. When I thought about my appointment, I reframed negative thoughts into positive ones and assured myself that I would be okay. I also reframed my immunotherapy treatment appointment as my wellness day. It made a huge difference. My husband used to come with me to the treatments and afterwards we'd go out for lunch and have a lovely day. I began to look forward to those days.

I was acting in alignment with who I wanted to be as a leader. I was being courageous, which is one of my top values. I repeated the process for every blood test, treatment and scan. I've had so many now that it's become routine – and that is the power of your mindset. It doesn't matter what you're faced with. Your mindset will influence your experience of it.

> YOUR MINDSET CAN BE YOUR SUPERPOWER.

A dictionary definition of 'mindset' is 'a person's way of thinking and their opinions'. I've distilled mindset into a model that I call the Inspired Mindset Model, and I'm going to share more about that with you soon.

In this chapter, I will show you that by adopting a solution-focused mindset, you can turn obstacles into opportunities and reframe negative thoughts into optimistic ones.

Siya Kolisi was the first black captain of the South African rugby team. He epitomises what I am going to share with you.

Growing up in a small and very poor town in South Africa, Siya experienced violence and poverty. His favourite toy was a brick. When his mother passed away when he was only 15, he was raised by his grandmother, who was a strong role model for him.

Siya started playing rugby at age seven, and five years later was offered a scholarship to the acclaimed Grey College – a 'white' school. He didn't speak any English at the time. He not only embraced the opportunity, he pushed through the many challenges to eventually make the South African rugby team and become the first black captain.

Siya's story is one of courage and resilience. It proves that we all have choices in life, no matter what. Siya could have chosen to see his situation as an barrier and remain in a cycle of poverty. Instead, he fought the limiting belief of 'I'm not good enough'. He chose to rise up against it. He has now written his autobiography, *Rise*, and chooses to use his stature and voice to create change.

Your mindset is malleable. It can change. It needs to be malleable if you want to grow in life. By using the Inspired Mindset Model, you can determine the mindset that you need to achieve any outcome or result. This is empowering. You can reframe thoughts, beliefs and ideas that are holding you back to ones that inspire you and propel you forward.

There are typically two types of mindsets, as described and popularised by renowned author Carol Dweck. She's a psychologist and

Stanford University professor as well as the best-selling author of *Mindset: The New Psychology of Success*. While I'm not going to go into the details of her work, I'm building on her theories around mindset with the Inspired Mindset Model.

You have a choice to influence your mindset; I will show you how in this chapter. I'll also show you some strategies to turn negative thoughts into positive ones and how to use these strategies to build resilience in the face of challenges and adversity. How you think about the life you want will largely determine whether you can achieve that. That is the power of your mind. By thinking that you can lead a life that you love, you are empowering yourself to take the actions needed to make it happen.

THE POWER OF THE MIND

Your mindset is incredibly powerful. According to Stanford University's Dr Jacob Towery, you see your life through your own unique lens.[2] This is your mindset – the assumptions and expectations that you hold about yourself, your life and the situations around you. Research shows that mindset plays a significant role in determining your life outcomes.

Dr Towery also says:

> *There is a powerful phenomenon in medicine known as the placebo effect, in which if someone believes they are going to derive benefits from taking a particular medication, they often do. In fact, regardless of the disease or condition, about 30–40% of people can have significant improvement in their symptoms even when taking a placebo (sugar) pill, if they believe that the pill is going to be helpful.*

Dr Towery also points out the impact of the 'nocebo-effect', a psychological response based on a person's expectations around side effects. When a physician emphasises the potential side effects of a medicine and the patient believes they will develop those symptoms, they may do so – even if they're given a sugar pill. Science is just beginning to validate the power of the mind-body relationship.

The power of mindset also has roots in ancient history. Philosophers such as Aristotle explored the importance of cultivating a virtuous mindset and the role of reason in leading a fulfilling and meaningful life. These philosophers emphasised the connection between mindset, personal ethics and the pursuit of wellbeing. In simple words, being virtuous starts with your mindset. A virtuous mindset will lead you to do the right thing; that is, if you're a good person, you will lead a good life. You have the power to change your mindset and, when you do, you can change your actions, and that changes your outcomes.

It is critical to take note of your mindset and ensure it's one that is empowering you. Your mindset influences your mind, body and soul. Your mindset arises from your beliefs and thoughts. Sometimes these beliefs and thoughts are conscious, which is great because you can use your rational mind to weigh up your situation. For example, you might think 'I'm a great cook', but then your rational mind can jump in and say, 'Just because I think I'm a great cook, that doesn't mean that I should dispense with recipes – I'd better find some to follow for tomorrow's dinner party.' Sometimes these beliefs and thoughts are subconscious, meaning they happen without you being aware of them. For example, when it's raining in the morning, I might subconsciously think 'It's too wet and cold to go to gym today.' I'll then stay in bed – and regret it later.

My unconscious thinking influenced my behaviour, which led to regret. That didn't help me at all.

By understanding, adapting and shifting your mindset, you can improve your health, decrease your anxiety and become more resilient to life's challenges.

You might be thinking, 'I have tried this before and it doesn't work.' Or even, 'Are you telling me that I am to blame for my problems? That if I had a better mindset, I wouldn't be sick or I wouldn't have lost my job?' I'm certainly not suggesting that you are to blame for all of your problems or difficulties. What I am saying is that you have a choice in how you handle the situation you're in. Remember, you can't control what happens to you, but you can control how you respond – that is the power of your mindset. I encourage you to try again. Working on your mindset can change how you experience things. I'm also about to show you a simple, practical model that will help you.

Think about a situation that you feel stuck in or a habit that you want to break. Reflect on what you 'think' about this situation or habit. Are your thoughts positive or negative? You can refer to the model in chapter 3 for help. Consider if you're solution-focused or stuck in the negative and believing that nothing you do will change your situation. You might be stuck in the habit of snacking and it's something that you want to break. Do you believe that you can break this habit, or are you thinking that you've got no control over it and that while a fridge or a cupboard still remains in your house, you are always going to find something to snack on? Write it down for now, we'll come back to it.

Sometimes people don't like reflecting on things because it makes them feel helpless, but I will show you how to change that feeling of helplessness to one of empowerment as we go through this chapter.

THE INSPIRED MINDSET MODEL

Now that you have more insight into the role your mindset plays in your choices, I'd like to introduce you to the Inspired Mindset Model. The Inspired Mindset Model is a leadership framework I developed to help you be intentional with your thoughts and actions to get your desired result. It's a practical way to help you align what you want to achieve with your mindset and actions.

Imagine your life as an iceberg, just like the ones Ernest Hemingway talked about. Most of the iceberg is hidden underwater, unseen but strong. That's where you get 90 per cent of your strength. Above the water, you see the tip, which is only 10 per cent of the whole thing.

In life, the 10 per cent above the water represents the outcomes and results you can see – what others notice about you. But your real power lies in the 90 per cent below the surface – the behaviours, decisions, thoughts, attitudes and beliefs that shape who you are (see figure 3).

Understanding this is essential. It means that to make real changes and be strong, you need to focus on the 90 per cent that others can't see. Strengthen your thoughts, attitudes and beliefs, and you'll have a solid foundation for success and happiness in life.

At the bottom of the model, you'll find the most crucial part – your mindset. Just like a building needs a strong foundation to stand tall, your mindset is the foundation of your strength. If you ensure your mindset is in the right place, this will boost your strength and resilience, just like a well-built foundation supports a sturdy building. Getting your mindset right is incredibly important for your overall growth and success because it influences your actions. For example, if you think you are not good enough to step up into a leadership position, you will not take the steps to pursue it.

Figure 3: The Inspired Mindset Model

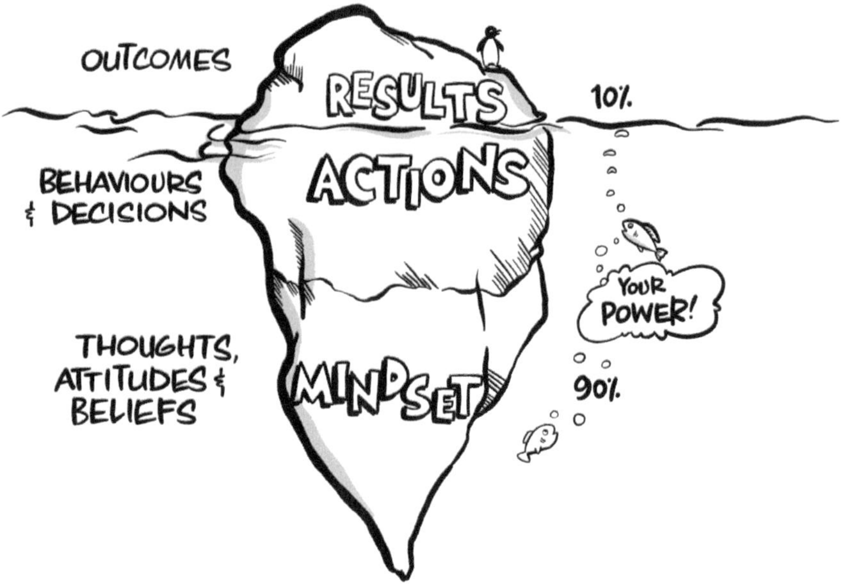

OUTCOMES — RESULTS — 10%

BEHAVIOURS & DECISIONS — ACTIONS

THOUGHTS, ATTITUDES & BELIEFS — MINDSET — 90%

YOUR POWER!

Your actions are the steps you take and the behaviours you exhibit as a result of your thinking. Depending on your mindset, how you behave and the action you take or don't take is a result of what you are thinking. This in turn influences your results, which has a direct impact on your life.

Roger Bannister was an English neurologist and middle-distance runner. His goal was to break the four-minute mile. For many years, 'experts' said that running a mile in under four minutes was impossible. Then on 6 May 1954, Roger did what was thought unattainable and ran the mile in 3 minutes 59.4 seconds.

It was only after Roger Bannister's record-breaking run that many other runners also ran the mile in under four minutes. (Today, the world record time for running the mile is 3 minutes 43.13 seconds.) What Bannister did was to break the self-imposed barrier that all runners had in their minds. This wasn't a physical barrier, it was a mental one. It took him eight years of part-time training to do it, but he believed he could. So he did.

There've been many situations in my life and in my clients' lives where this model has been incredibly beneficial. One of my downfalls is snacking in the afternoon. It's a bad habit I got into when I started working from home more often. Unobstructed access to the fridge and the cupboard was at my fingertips. It was a distraction for me. So, I would get up many times in the afternoon believing I was hungry. The problem was I wasn't snacking on an apple, celery or something else that would give me energy to get through the day. It was bread and lots of peanut butter (my weakness). This belief that I was hungry in the afternoon and needed to constantly snack wasn't working for me.

I sat down and worked out how I could reframe this mindset that led to snacking on unhelpful foods to establish a snacking routine of yoghurt and strawberries, and ensuring these were readily available. Once I had reframed my mindset to the choice of healthy wholefoods as opposed to quick and easy bread and peanut better as a snack, my shopping habits changed and the results reflected this. I felt better in my body and my energy levels improved too. Did I slip up? Of course. But as you will understand as you read further on, my focus is progress, not perfection. The slip-ups happened less and less often. That is a simple example of how the Inspired Mindset Model can work.

You might think it seems like a lot of hard work to think this way, or wonder what will happen if you forget the model in the heat of the moment. I totally get that, and coming up is a great little hack to remember the model. It also doesn't matter if you forget it in the moment. What matters is that you can use the model to self-reflect, then learn from the situation and perhaps decide on a better way of approaching it next time.

A hack: reversing the Inspired Mindset Model

If you get stuck using the Inspired Mindset Model or are having trouble applying it, reverse it. Start at the top and think about your outcome first. Then move to the bottom. What mindset do you need to adopt and what actions and behaviours do you need to implement to achieve that outcome? For example, you might want to stop eating Tim Tams and eat an apple instead. That is your outcome. What's the mindset that you need to adopt? It might be one of health. It might be one of 'I choose the apple because it's sweet and good for me.' Then, what actions do you need to implement? It might be you don't walk down the biscuit aisle in the supermarket so that you don't buy Tim Tams anymore, and you make a point of buying apples instead so they are always available.

For those of you who are outcome-driven like I am, this really helps. This hack is a framework that you can use to think about the result that you desire first and then align your mindset and behaviour to that. You can use this for your leadership, your personal brand, changing a habit, improving your health or whatever result you're after. You can also use this model to reframe a negative thought.

Imagine a child learning to walk. They see others walking and get very curious and start to believe they can do it too. With determination, they take action, even if they stumble and fall along the way. It doesn't deter them; they keep trying until they achieve their goal of walking.

It's not a guaranteed method, but when you grasp this concept, it becomes a powerful tool to influence the outcomes and results you want. Understanding this allows you to align your mindset and actions with the outcomes you desire. Just like that determined child, you can keep pushing forward until you achieve success.

My ultimate goal is to be cancer-free. While I understand that I can't control the outcome entirely, I firmly believe that I can influence it by taking proactive steps. This strong belief drives my actions.

Having a positive mindset has become my driving force. I choose to believe in my ability to overcome this challenge, and that shapes the decisions I make. I've gained clarity on my priorities, boundaries, and what supports my mental and physical wellbeing. I'm selective about the people I surround myself with and what I expose myself to, all fuelled by my determination to be cancer-free.

This mindset empowers me to make informed choices about what I do and don't do. I've reframed my thinking to reject the notion of impossibility, as believing that I can't be cancer-free would only lead me down a dark path. Instead, I focus on the belief that I am here to live, and I will live to the fullest while I can.

Everyone's motivations differ, but for me, being cancer-free is my motivation and inspiration. I am committed to doing everything within my control to achieve this goal. It may be a challenging road, but I'm ready to face it with determination and strength.

By understanding what I want to achieve and aligning my mindset and actions with that goal, I feel empowered and motivated to keep moving forward. I won't let the fear of the unknown hold me back. Instead, I embrace a mindset that serves me, propelling me towards the life I envision – a life free from cancer.

You might think, 'What if the outcome I want is something beyond my control?', or you might not believe that this framework can help you at the click of a finger. You're right: it will take work. In the next section, I will show you how to reframe your thoughts.

Using the example that you are working on for this chapter, ask yourself the following questions and write down the answers:

- What do you need to believe about the situation you wrote down?
- What mindset do you want to adopt?
- Are there thoughts that you need to change in order to achieve your result?
- What actions do you need to take to achieve your desired result?

REFRAMING NEGATIVE SELF-TALK

Now that you understand the power of the Inspired Mindset Model, you can use it to reframe negative self-talk. You can also use it when others are imposing their limiting beliefs on you.

Negative self-talk refers to inner dialogue or thoughts that are critical, self-deprecating or pessimistic about yourself. It describes the habit of consistently using harsh and discouraging language towards yourself, often leading to feelings of inadequacy, low self-esteem, and self-doubt.

Negative self-talk can manifest in various ways, such as:

- *Self-criticism:* Constantly berating yourself for perceived flaws or mistakes, often using phrases such as 'I'm so stupid' or 'I can't do anything right.'

- *Catastrophising*: Exaggerating potential negative outcomes or expecting the worst in every situation, leading to increased anxiety and fear.
- *Filtering*: Focusing solely on negative aspects while ignoring positive ones, leading to a skewed and pessimistic view of yourself and your life.
- *Blame*: Blaming yourself for things that are beyond your control or assuming responsibility for events that are not your fault.
- *Comparison*: Constantly measuring yourself against others and feeling inadequate, or envious of their achievements. (This is very common.)
- *Labelling*: Attaching negative labels to yourself based on past mistakes or shortcomings, such as 'I'm a failure' or 'I'm worthless.'

Negative self-talk can be damaging to your mental and emotional wellbeing, impacting your confidence, motivation and overall life satisfaction. It's essential to recognise and challenge negative self-talk, and cultivate positive and compassionate self-talk, which fosters self-acceptance and growth.

The power of reframing lies in its ability to shift our perspective and change the way we interpret situations, events or challenges. Reframing often involves looking at a situation from a different angle or adopting an alternative viewpoint that can bring about new insights, opportunities and positive outcomes.

In his book *The Seven Habits of Highly Effective People*, Stephen Covey shares a great example of this. He wrote that he was sitting on a train on Sunday morning in New York. It was calm and peaceful, with some passengers resting their eyes or reading a newspaper.

Then suddenly a man entered the carriage with his children. The children were loud and disruptive. The man sat next to Covey and closed his eyes. He was apparently oblivious to what his children were doing. They were yelling, throwing things and even grabbing at people's papers. But the man sitting next to him did nothing. This irritated Covey. He couldn't understand why the man took no responsibility and did nothing about his children's very obvious poor behaviour. Covey saw that others on the train felt irritated too.

Eventually, he turned to the man and said, 'Sir, your children are really disturbing a lot of people. I wonder if you could control them a little more?' The man lifted his gaze and said, 'Oh, you're right. I guess I should do something about it. We've just come from the hospital where their mother died about an hour ago. I don't know what to think or do and I guess they don't know how to handle it either.'

Covey asks if we can imagine how he felt. Once the man explained to him why his kids were behaving that way, Covey reframed the situation immediately from something negative to one deserving compassion. He saw things differently, thought differently and then behaved differently. He was able to put himself in someone else's shoes.

You may find yourself automatically assigning a negative belief to a situation, whether about others or yourself, and your actions will reflect that. Reframing allows you to reinterpret the meaning you have assigned. By reframing, you can transform a negative or challenging circumstance into a learning experience or an opportunity for growth. It's a chance to develop resilience. Reframing helps you find the silver lining in difficult situations and view setbacks as stepping stones to success.

You can reframe the negative self-talk that holds you back and keeps you stuck to something that is empowering and positive. You can do this by using the Inspired Mindset Model I showed you earlier. Using the Inspired Mindset Model is a reliable way, a memorable way, to reframe negative self-talk.

A client of mine, Lisa, is a talented artist with a passion for painting. She dreamed of showcasing her artwork in a local gallery but battled with negative self-talk. Whenever she picked up a brush, a relentless voice in her head would say, 'You're not good enough. No one will like your art.'

Her self-doubt grew with every stroke, causing her to hide her paintings away, afraid of rejection. She received compliments from friends, but convinced herself they were just being polite.

When we started working together, I shared the Inspired Mindset Model with her and empowered her to reframe her negative self-talk into positive affirmations. With encouragement, instead of listening to her inner critic, she reminded herself, 'I am talented, and my art deserves to be seen.'

As Lisa's self-talk shifted, so did her confidence. She mustered the courage to submit her paintings to a gallery. To her surprise, they were accepted, and her artwork received admiration from visitors.

By reframing her negative self-talk, Lisa realised her true potential. She embraced her creativity and gained the recognition she deserved. From that day forward, she learned the power of positive self-talk, allowing her talent to shine brightly in the world. You can do this too. Your work, your voice, your art deserves and needs to be seen.

REFRAMING EXTERNAL LIMITING BELIEFS

Throughout my life, I've encountered others who imposed limiting beliefs on me. People often don't realise the power of their words and how they can affect others. During my cancer journey, I faced doctors repeatedly telling me bleak things – that my cancer might come back, that remission was unlikely, and that I would have to choose between treatment and quality of life. Hearing this was incredibly detrimental to my mental health and hope.

It made me feel defeated and sad. I questioned why those who should believe in me doubted my ability to overcome this challenge. Why wouldn't they want me to be a positive statistic instead of accepting a less hopeful outcome? It tested my resilience, and I couldn't comprehend why they kept using this language with me. When I asked one of my doctors, she explained it was about managing expectations, but I requested her not to use that language with me because it made me feel disempowered. I needed her to believe in me.

I didn't let others' words define me. In each situation, I took the power of reframing into my hands. I changed 'I can't beat this' to 'I will beat this,' and I made a commitment to do everything in my power to overcome this challenge.

This kind of language imposition occurs in many other circumstances. In our formative years, careless remarks from parents or teachers can shape our beliefs about ourselves, affecting our actions and potential. This can extend into adulthood if we are not aware.

Reframing is a powerful tool. It helps you challenge and change limiting beliefs – your own or those imposed on you – empowering you to take control of your life and pursue your goals with determination. By recognising the impact of language on your mindset, you can cultivate a positive and resilient outlook, breaking free from the limitations others might try to place on you.

You might be thinking, 'I've been talking to myself this way for years, for my whole life. It's too simplistic to think I can change my beliefs now.' But you might be surprised how much reframing can help you be more proactive in challenging situations rather than reacting. Reframing helps you open your eyes to alternate perspectives and achieve personal growth. The exception is when there is a serious situation – for example, bullying, sexual harassment or criminal behaviour. These are difficult situations and often not for reframing. If you are involved in any of these scenarios, take the appropriate action and report it, and seek professional support.

Look at the example that you're working on in this chapter. Choose one negative belief, thought or interpretation about what you're trying to change that you can reframe to be more solution-focused. Use the Inspired Mindset Model for this. Think about the outcome that you want to achieve. How can you reframe it to be something more empowering? What can you learn from this situation? Write it down. You might struggle to do this because you can't think positively about the situation. Imagine that you could. What might you think or believe, or what might you suggest to your best friend if they had a similar issue to the one that you are working on?

CONCLUSION

In this chapter we've looked at the remarkable influence of your mindset and how you can use it as your superpower. It is something that can either hinder your progress or propel you forward. The

Inspiring Mindset Model will become a tool that you refer to constantly. It could be one of the most powerful tools in your toolkit like it is in mine, similar to the above the line and below the line model. Regardless of gender or age, we're all innate meaning-makers capable of reframing the significance that we assign to situations, using the model. This newfound awareness empowers you to learn valuable lessons from what happens in your life and can support your growth significantly.

Start using the Inspired Mindset Model as a tool to determine your mindset, influence your behaviours and help you to change them. You can change your life and make sure that you're leading a life that you love. Stop thinking that your mind controls you, because you have more power than you think.

In the next chapter, I will show you something that will have a huge impact on your life. I will shine a light on resilience and show you how to connect to the authentic leader in you by anchoring yourself so that you can live a life of alignment and experience happiness.

Chapter 6

BUILDING YOUR RESILIENCE

Anchoring yourself to who you are and building resilience go hand in hand. Building resilience requires a deep understanding of who you are – your values, beliefs, strengths and passions. Knowing who you are and what is important to you provides you with a guiding light to make strong choices and live in alignment with your values and aspirations. It also enables you to tap into your inner strengths in the face of adversity.

Just as a tree stands firm against strong winds, knowing who you are at the core acts as your anchor, allowing you to weather life's storms with resilience. Like the roots of a tree, your core identity provides stability, confidence and a sense of purpose.

> BY UNDERSTANDING AND EMBRACING THE FUNDAMENTALS OF YOU, YOU CAN CULTIVATE THE INNER STRENGTH NEEDED TO NAVIGATE CHALLENGES AND BOUNCE BACK FROM ADVERSITY.

When I received my cancer diagnosis, it was a massive shock that shook my confidence to the core. Facing something beyond my control was a true test of my strength like nothing else. Fitness and health were once integral to my identity, but now, I found myself grappling with stage three melanoma cancer – an aggressive and, by definition, unwelcome change.

In the face of this unfamiliar and daunting territory, I sought answers from doctors and oncologists, needing to hear those reassuring words, 'You'll be okay.' But that validation never came. The absence of those words left me feeling defeated and hopeless – emotions I despised.

Determined not to let fear overpower me, I chose to reclaim my confidence. As I described in chapter 5, I envisioned the outcome I desired, using the Inspired Mindset Model in reverse, and rediscovered my true self. I reconnected with my core values: courage and strength. No longer willing to be at the mercy of circumstances, I took charge and determined my actions. In doing so, I created my own hope and implemented strategies that proved vital for supporting my mental wellbeing in the face of adversity.

Now, I want to share these empowering strategies with you. In this chapter, we'll delve into finding your guiding light – unearthing your top three values. We'll explore how living in alignment with these values becomes an anchor for building resilience. We'll uncover what you truly stand for and what you stand against. Together, we'll engage in a powerful exercise that will illuminate your path further.

Resilience will be our guiding theme; we'll uncover the steps to build your resilience amid life's challenges. As you embrace these practical insights and exercises, you'll find the strength to face any obstacle head-on, just as I did. The journey towards hope, courage and strength starts here.

FINDING YOUR GUIDING LIGHT

Your top three values act as a guiding light for your life, illuminating the way forward for you. They provide you with a sense of direction or purpose. When you live in alignment with your values, you feel a sense of authenticity, integrity and happiness.

You might have more than three values and that's okay, but anchoring yourself to three is something that you can easily embed into your mind. Our brains naturally gravitate towards threes. The Latin phrase 'Omne trium perfectum,' which translates to 'Everything that comes in threes is perfect,' implies that presenting things in threes not only creates a strong impression but can also have a lasting impact on the human mind. Think, for example, of the phrases 'sex, drugs and rock and roll' or 'blood, sweat and tears'. These phrases are easy to remember. This powerful pattern highlights the profound connection between our thoughts and actions. By recognising this simplicity, we can harness its potential to easily make positive changes in our lives.

Your values will change and evolve as you grow. They can also shift when certain life events happen. They can be fluid, but there are some that remain core.

Your values are the things you believe to be very important; that shape how you live and work. They reflect your priorities (or they should!) and serve as a measure of whether your life is aligned with what truly matters to you.

When your actions and behaviours align with your values, life feels satisfying and content. However, when there's a disconnect between your choices and your values, a sense of unease and unhappiness arises.

For example, if you value family yet your career demands you work 60 hours a week and takes you away from those you love most, will you be happy? If you value harmonious relationships yet you work in a very unsettled and competitive environment where people are pitted against each other, do you think you'll thrive?

This is why it's crucial to consciously identify our values. Doing so makes life easier as we can align our plans and decisions accordingly. Once you explore your values, clarity emerges, leading to better decisions and a sense of purpose.

Values, like respect, play a significant role in our lives. When you live out of alignment with them, frustration and confusion occur. It's easy to become disconnected from your values simply because you're juggling too many balls and getting trapped in busy. This leads to overwhelm and the realisation that your life is not how you want it. I've witnessed this with my clients, too – when their values clash with a situation, emotions run high.

My client Jessie needed to advocate for herself to be considered for senior leadership positions. She worked in a male-dominated industry and faced many obstacles to achieving her goal. Jessie's leader at the time didn't consider her ready and wasn't championing her. Rather than giving up, we worked to reconnect Jessie to her value of determination and worked up a strategy for her to demonstrate her abilities. It certainly wasn't easy, but embodying determination helped her move forward rather than resign to the situation and give up her dream. Jessie got that role. It took her some time, but she never gave up.

> **LIVING IN ALIGNMENT WITH YOUR VALUES IS A GAME-CHANGER.**

Throughout my cancer journey, knowing my true self has been crucial in facing challenges head-on. It has empowered me to advocate for myself, even when I felt overwhelmed, and embrace my identity despite the difficulties. Whether it's a major hurdle or a minor setback I'm facing, connecting with my values allows me to stand strong and stay true to who I am.

In December 2021 I had some scans following my first immunotherapy treatment. It was thought my cancer would come back quickly because it was considered aggressive. My oncologist was on leave, so I saw another to get the results. He told me that my cancer had returned, not only in my pelvic area where the cancer had initially spread, but on my lungs and bones. My husband and I were devastated. I honestly felt that I only had a very limited time to live. The treatment hadn't worked and my enemy within was winning.

However, when my back is against the wall, the best in me comes out. The enemy would not beat me! I anchored myself to my value of courage. I contacted my surgeon, who I was still consulting with, and asked for his opinion. He provided me with a very different perspective. He explained that the scans were certainly not conclusive. As my body was still recovering from surgery, certain 'activity' would be expected to show up, and the next scans would be a better indication of what was really going on. My surgeon gave me hope! That was all I needed.

These two very different conversations highlight two things – the power of language and how words have a huge impact; and how showing empathy in a situation can make an enormous difference to the outcome. It was quite possible that my cancer had spread, *but* it was a possibility, not definitive. It also highlighted a third thing: the power of choice. I had a choice to accept it or not. Being anchored to who I am made it easier to challenge what I was hearing and find solutions.

You might wonder how adaptability fits with holding onto your values. Adaptability is vital since change is constant. However, being connected to your values enhances your ability to navigate change. Anchoring yourself in your core values provides strength and resilience when facing challenges.

James Clear, author of *Atomic Habits*, says 'let your values drive your choices'. When he is working on a problem in his business, he first asks, 'will the solution fit my values?'. Then he asks, 'is the solution aligned with my goals?'. If the answer to either questions is no, he looks for an alternate solution.

There may be situations where you need to compromise a value. For example, say you highly value honesty and integrity in your relationships. You believe in always telling the truth and being transparent with your loved ones. However, you find yourself in a situation where a close friend confides in you about a secret that could potentially harm someone else. In this instance, you face a moral dilemma between your commitment to honesty and loyalty to your friend. You choose to compromise the value of honesty by not revealing the secret, putting your friendship above honesty. This is a conscious choice made as you have assessed the pros and cons. It happens – the important thing is you made an empowered decision.

Here's an exercise for you to uncover your top three values:

1. Carve out time for reflection. Do you know what your top three values are? If you don't, reflect on your priorities in life.

Health, family, adventure, joy or balance, for example? Write these down.

2. Consider times when you have felt moments of fulfilment and happiness. What was it about these moments that made you happy? What were you doing? Who were you with? What do you constantly get feedback about? Are you a great listener or communicator? Do you make people feel valued? Are you funny or fun? Write these down.

3. Think about a time where you've been frustrated, hurt or angry. What was it about the situation that made you angry? Was someone dishonest? Did you feel disrespected? Was someone unkind? Did they not show up on time? Did they make you feel unsafe? Write these down. (Chances are, your values are the opposite of these.)

4. Reflect on where you spend your money. That can give you a good indication of what you value, too.

5. Reflect on a role model, someone you admire. What do you admire about them? Is it their strength? Do they walk their talk? Are they kind? Are they a good listener, curious or successful?

6. Review what you have written, and circle the three values that resonate the strongest for you. I encourage you not to overthink this. Go with what feels right for you.

If you're still not identifying the values that feel like 'you', the following examples may help: integrity, honesty, joy, freedom, achievement, connection, certainty, inspiration, happiness, wealth.

My clients often find this exercise challenging. Often when we are thinking introspectively and deeply it can be, but it's worth it.

Your values evolve and change as you grow. Follow the process and if you are finding it difficult the next section of this chapter may help.

WHAT DO YOU STAND FOR AND AGAINST?

Understanding what you want to be known for and what you stand against involves reflecting on the legacy you wish to leave behind. This goes beyond personal values and extends to the impact that you want to have on others and the world. Defining your legacy is an important part of living a life you love. It's also strongly related to the power of values in shaping the impact you have on others and the world.

Once you have clarity around what you stand for and against, this supports you in making choices, setting goals and ensuring your actions align with your desired legacy. Ultimately this leads to a more fulfilling and purpose-driven life, one that you are proud of. It enables you to anchor yourself in the face of adversity.

I stand firmly against animal cruelty, and it's a value I will never compromise on, no matter where I am in the world. Take, for instance, the popular elephant rides in Asia – I will never participate in such activities. To me, it's inhumane and cruel to exploit these majestic creatures for human pleasure. Even the thought of it leaves me emotional. Similarly, I'm appalled by the mistreatment of tigers in some places, where they are drugged and kept docile for petting. Zoos, too, don't sit well with me. I believe wild animals belong in their natural habitat, free to roam and thrive. Seeing them locked up in cages saddens me deeply.

These beliefs are at the core of who I am, and I remain steadfast in upholding them. While I don't judge others who have different perspectives, I personally choose not to partake in such activities. Instead, I channel my passion into supporting organisations that work to end animal cruelty. It's my way of standing up for what I believe in.

This was a challenge when I was engaged to be the motivational speaker at an event in Malaysia. In an activity that was part of the event, we were challenged to break through a fear barrier and hold a snake. The snake was kept in a bag and was very docile. Doing this went against what I stood for, but I was the 'motivational speaker' at the event so I felt some pressure to participate. In the end I decided not to partake and the organisers didn't respond well. However, I would not support an activity that I believed was cruel. I wasn't invited to speak at the event again, but I felt proud to have made an empowering decision in line with my values. I have not once regretted my decision.

Now, I ask you, what values do you hold close to your heart? What do you stand for, and what do you stand against? These guiding principles define us and influence our actions. Embrace them, for they shape the person you are and the positive impact you can make in the world.

A good friend of mine stands for pet health. She's a huge advocate for it and has created a business that educates people and provides treats and supplements that support dogs and cats. She works tirelessly and I'm so proud of her. Not only because it's aligned with a belief of mine and what I stand for, but because she passionately stands for what she believes in and what she has learned by having her own dog that she adores. She wants to prolong his life and help others who want to do the same.

Tuning into bigger causes than your own happiness and wellbeing helps to keep you going when times are tough. It can help to think beyond your own troubles and create the ripple effects of change that you want to see in the world. It's powerful.

Pablo Picasso was one of the most renowned artists of the 20th century and is one of my favourites. He had specific aspirations regarding how he wanted to be known and what he didn't want to be known for. Generally, Picasso wanted to be known for innovation, versatility and artistic revolution. You'll see that influence reflected in all of his art, such as different styles of paintings, illustrations, sculptures and ceramics. What he didn't want to be known for was conformity and predictability. He once said, 'If I paint a wild horse, you might not see the horse, but surely you will see the wildness.' He lived, worked and created in alignment with who he was authentically, and he left a remarkable impact on the world.

You might be thinking, 'I've never really been a person who stands for something.' If this is you, your causes might be highly personal. They might be about gardening or about painting. You might do community work or contribute to causes that are important to you. It's different for everyone.

WHAT DO YOU WANT TO BE KNOWN FOR?

In the example I shared above, you can see I remained true to what I stood for and against. My decision was also linked to what I want to be known for. I want to be known as someone who walks their talk, who is courageous, who uses her voice and is a role model for others to do the same. If I had taken part in the activity of holding the snake, I would not only have been a hypocrite but confused the people who know me and what I stand for. I refuse to do that.

You may get a feel in reading this book that I am strongly anchored to who I am and what I stand for. This didn't just happen, though – it took a lot of self-reflection, self-awareness and courage – of course! I learned about the power of legacy very early on in my leadership career. We often link legacy to death.

> **YOUR LEGACY ISN'T SOMETHING THAT YOU CREATE ON YOUR DEATHBED, THOUGH; IT'S SOMETHING THAT YOU CREATE EVERY SINGLE DAY THROUGH YOUR ACTIONS AND DECISIONS.**

It's the impact you leave on the world. I believe we need to be thinking about that now – not leaving it to chance or a time when you are experiencing a crisis. You have the power to influence your legacy.

You leave a legacy when you leave a job, for example. People remember you in a certain way. The question is, is it the way you want to be remembered?

During my corporate career I wanted to go for a big leadership role. When I went to speak to my leader about stepping up and taking the promotion, he did not consider that I was leadership material. I saw myself as a leader who would be a great fit for that role. He didn't. I couldn't understand why until I asked people I trusted for feedback. They gave me feedback that I didn't like. They shared that I was positioning myself as someone who was fun, the life of the party, who didn't take life too seriously. That might be great in a personal sense, but it wasn't the perception I was trying to create at work. I considered myself to be responsible, dedicated and diligent, performing extremely well.

I had to take a good hard look in the mirror and accept my reality. It was a difficult time in my life, but certainly important. It was one of the most valuable lessons I learned and one I now share freely.

I had to realign my behaviours back to who I was and what I stood for. I'd fallen into the trap of behaving in a way others wanted me to. It wasn't working for me. It took me a year to change people's perceptions, but I did it. I finally got that role! That's the power of understanding what you want to be known for.

THE POWER OF THREE WORDS

The exercise I'm about to share with you is one of the best to align your actions to a life that you want to live. It's something that I do every single year, and most of my clients who do this believe it's worth its weight in gold.

The exercise is called three words. Working through it can provide you with valuable insights into how others perceive you and whether this is aligned to the legacy and impact you want to create.

I will warn you up front: this exercise can be confronting and will require a sense of bravery. Anything this deeply personal does. However, it's a powerful exploratory and self-awareness tool that will help you endlessly.

Here are the steps:

1. Write down three words that you would use to describe yourself. Don't overthink it. What do you think people would say about you if you weren't in the room?

2. Ask three people that you respect and trust to give you the honest truth. Ask them to choose three words they would use to describe you and why. The best people to ask are those who you work with or have worked with, or who you've known for a long time. Avoid asking family members or close friends unless they're brutally honest. This is about hearing the truth. Explain why you are doing this exercise. You might say you are

wanting to check in on how you are perceived, increase your self-awareness or improve your leadership or personal brand. It's important for the person providing you with feedback that they understand the purpose.

3. This is important: when you receive the feedback, graciously accept it. Do not argue about it. Asking others to do this for you can be confronting for them also. They may be worried about upsetting you. Put them at ease.

4. Once you get their feedback, see if your perception of yourself and what others think of you is similar. Are people describing you differently to how you described yourself? Are you happy with how others perceive you? Are there consistencies between what you think and what they think? This can highlight whether you are adjusting your behaviour according to who you are with, like I was.

5. Now that you have this information, consider your aspirations and how you want to be known. Do you need to realign your actions and behaviours to achieve this? I highly recommend you use the Inspired Mindset Model to help you with this. That is where I started too. Once I got clarity on how I wanted to be perceived (my result), I could determine my mindset and actions accordingly. *Caveat:* any changes to your behaviour must be authentic to who you truly are, and in line with your values. You can't be someone you are not at the core. For example, you can't suddenly decide to be a hardcore sports fan if you don't enjoy sports. It just won't work because it's not aligned with who you are.

It takes a big dose of courage to do this but I'm always grateful to have gone through this exercise. Often we think we're being perceived one way, yet the reality is quite different. You might think you don't care what other people perceive of you, but I honestly believe that if that were the case, you wouldn't be reading this book.

Be brave. Explain to those you're asking for feedback how you're feeling and ask them to frame the feedback with kindness and compassion.

YOUR HIDDEN STRENGTH IN TIMES OF CHANGE AND ADVERSITY

To be resilient, you first need to understand what it means and how you can tap into it when you face a challenge. The dictionary definition of resilience is 'the capacity to withstand or recover quickly from difficulties or toughness'. In other words, resilience is the ability to adapt – to bounce back and recover from adversity, challenges or stressful situations. It's your capacity to withstand and overcome difficulties, setbacks such as losing your job, or traumatic experiences such as the death of a loved one. It's your capacity to maintain mental, emotional and physical wellbeing in the face of adversity, as we discussed in chapter 1.

You can build resilience by adopting the strategies that I've shared with you in the previous chapters, particularly in chapter 5 via the power of your mindset. Being anchored to your values and who you are gives you strength too.

> REMEMBER, YOU CAN'T CONTROL WHAT HAPPENS TO YOU BUT YOU CAN CONTROL HOW YOU RESPOND. THIS IS THE POWER OF RESILIENCE.

I am confident that you will have faced challenges in the past, unless you have lived a very charmed life. They may have been big or small but the important thing is you got through those challenges. Your darkness eventually became light and you felt better again. Reflecting on these situations will give you confidence that you've done it before and you can do it again.

You might imagine a bridge connecting you to a brighter future. To withstand the weight of challenges, this bridge needs to have two sturdy pillars: resilience and self-awareness. Resilience serves as a structure that enables you to bounce back. Knowing how to build it ensures the bridge's strength to help you reach the other side ready for what lies ahead. By actively tapping into your resilience, you can face change and adversity with greater strength, adaptability and confidence. You'll do this by focusing on solutions and approaching a situation with determination and persistence. You'll have a 'never give up' attitude when you need it.

I am constantly facing challenging situations. Constantly! As I'm sure you are too. Even while writing this, I had to dig deep into my resilience. Right in the middle of my writing, I received news that a painful side effect I was experiencing, caused by immunotherapy, was being worsened by the targeted tablet therapy I was taking. This was very hard to hear because, at the time, I thought if I couldn't tolerate the tablet therapy I'd be out of options. Repeating immunotherapy wasn't an option for me because of the extreme side effects I experience. It was suggested that I would need to consider my quality of life. While those words might seem reasonable, in the cancer world they can signal the end.

When I hung up the phone, I was understandably very emotional. I was angry that I was winning the challenge against the cancer, it was staying away, but the side effects of treatment were going to get me instead. I went into blame mode again and slipped into the mindset of 'poor me'. I asked myself, how many times can you get knocked down before you stay down? I was so fed up. I just wanted to crawl under my doona and never come out.

Eventually (and reluctantly), I regrouped and switched my mindset to solution mode. I asked to speak to my oncologist to discuss the situation and get her perspective. Thankfully, I found out I did have options.

People often ask me whether some of us are born strong and resilient. Many of the people I've worked with haven't considered themselves as resilient, or they've said something like, 'I used to be resilient, but that has changed. I haven't got the fight in me anymore.' I totally understand that. But resilience can be cultivated. Start by setting small challenges for yourself, such as going for an early morning walk if that's something you think you can't do, or even simply getting up and making your bed in the morning. It's the small steps that propel us forward. Start small and build up. I build resilience by looking for inspirational local stories where people demonstrate resilience in their situation. There are so many. I love finding out about people who have succeeded against the odds, those who have overcome enormous challenges, people like you and me. Hearing these stories inspires me to be more resilient when I face challenges. Especially when I feel like giving up.

There may be exceptional circumstances where understanding resilience may not be sufficient to overcome extreme and traumatic events that require specialised support, such as severe mental health conditions or very traumatic experiences. In that case, seek professional help from medical professionals.

To help you build resilience, follow this exercise:

1. Take time for self-reflection and identify challenging situations you've faced in the past.

2. Consider how you responded, what strengths you utilised and what you learned from those experiences. Write them down.
3. Reframe any negative or limiting beliefs about your resilience using the Inspired Mindset Model in chapter 5. How else can you think about this in the positive?
4. Challenge any self-doubt that might come up and shift yourself above the line. Get curious.
5. Make a list of your past successes and refer to it when you're feeling defeated or you don't have the fight anymore. This can give you confidence in your ability to handle the next challenge. You can always dig deeper than you think you can.

If you are doubting that you have been resilient and believe you just crumble and fall in a heap, ask a family member or a great friend to help you think through this exercise.

CONCLUSION

In this chapter, you've gained invaluable insights into identifying and embracing your core values while creating the legacy you envision. You now understand the significance of the three words that define you and how they shape your influence. You've come to appreciate the essence of resilience – how aligning with your values and convictions empowers you to build unwavering strength in the face of challenges. Stop letting others set your course in life because you don't know what matters to you. Start leading your life in alignment with what truly matters and create a legacy you're proud of.

Now that you know your core values, what you want to be known for and how to tap into your resilience, in the next chapter, I will show you how to have the courage to be the leader of you. I will show you how to step outside your comfort zone and unlock the confidence to lead a life you love. It's going to be awesome.

Chapter 7

HAVE THE COURAGE TO BE THE CEO OF YOU

Now that we've talked about all the elements needed to live a life you love, you must have the courage to realise it. Have the courage to be the CEO of you. You have reconnected to who you are and what you stand for – now it's about action.

Taking decisive action is what's needed to stretch beyond your comfort zone, break free of limitations and expand your horizons. Action brings the idea from a concept into reality. It gives you confidence. As you act, you realise you can mould your life to be what you want it to be, rather than allowing others to shape it for you. The best part is, this process will open up new opportunities for you, build resilience and help you lead a life you love.

Being the leader of you is like being the conductor of your own symphony. You are the conductor of your life, and the symphony is the life that you are orchestrating. You guide the musicians (representing various aspects of your life) to create a harmonious and meaningful composition. Just as a conductor sets the tempo, cues the musicians and brings together the different sections of the orchestra, as the leader of you, you set the pace and direction of your life. You make deliberate choices, establish priorities and harmonise the different elements of your life, such as how many balls you might juggle, your relationships, your career and your wellbeing. The conductor's role involves making decisions in real time, responding to the music and the musicians' performance. Similarly, as the leader of you, you need to adapt, make adjustments and respond to the ever-changing circumstances and challenges that arise. This takes courage.

 **LEADERSHIP IS ACTION.**

Taking decisive action to be the leader of you is to take deliberate and well-considered steps in line with your values and who you want to be as that leader. It's not taking the easy way out because you feel scared to do something or it seems too hard, it's making a decision to do it anyway.

As Maya Angelou once said, 'Stand up straight and realize who you are, that you tower over your circumstances.' The true essence of leadership is to act as you must, not as you feel. This is not about being a robot or feeling like you're at a bootcamp in the army. It's getting out of bed because you know it's good for you to go for a walk and you'll feel better having done it. It's speaking up in the meeting even though you're scared you'll get shut down, because you'll regret it if you don't. It's standing up for what you believe even when it's not the popular choice.

Life is full of difficult moments. It's full of challenges and disappointments. The true test of your character and of your leadership is how you respond to those challenges. Therein lies your decision. This brings the idea of leading your life, determining how many balls you juggle and leading above the line into your reality. You will quickly be able to move from being overwhelmed to being in control.

In her influential research on postural feedback, social psychologist Amy Cuddy explored the connection between body language, confidence and leadership. Her studies demonstrate that adopting certain poses – such as standing tall with an open posture – can increase feelings of confidence, reduce stress and enhance performance in challenging situations. By embodying these poses, people can tap into their inner courage and present themselves as more authoritative and influential leaders. While there has been some debate about the research because the results have not yet been replicated, I have certainly tried this theory out in my corporate career and in my business and seen the benefits. I recall when I presented my first keynote to a large audience. To say I felt scared is an understatement, but I wasn't going to run away! I remember pushing my shoulders back, standing tall and smiling. I certainly felt more confident through my improved posture. I encourage you to do the same now. If you are slouching or feeling low right now, sit or stand up straight, put a smile on your dial and hold your head up high. Can you feel it too?

In Cuddy's book, *Presence: Bringing Your Boldest Self to Your Biggest Challenges*, Cuddy delves deeper into the importance of embracing courage in personal leadership. She emphasises the concept of self-affirmation, which involves acknowledging and aligning with your core values, strengths and passions. By cultivating self-affirmation, we can strengthen our sense of self-worth and tap into our inner courage, enabling us to lead with authenticity and inspire others to follow. These insights from Cuddy's research provide compelling evidence that courage plays a vital role in personal leadership, empowering us to overcome challenges, exude confidence and make meaningful impact.

In this chapter, I will show you how to step outside of your comfort zone and make those important decisions. I will show you that using your voice is key and that courage, fear and confidence go hand in hand – you can't have one without the others. I'll also show you the importance of progress over perfection. I've mentioned this a lot in this book so far and will reiterate it again: what I'm sharing with you is not about being perfect. It's about progress. It's about embracing the Inspired Mindset Model, doing your best to live and lead above the line and embracing any mistakes and failures as learning opportunities.

DECIDE TO BE THE LEADER OF YOU

Deciding to be the leader of you and living a life you love often means shifting outside your comfort zone. It means changing what you've always done, such as juggling too many balls because you want to please others; not using your voice or not advocating for yourself because you worry about what others will think of you; and not wanting to explore other career opportunities because you don't feel you have the confidence. All of these things limit you from being the person you want to be and leading the life you love.

Imagine your comfort zone as a cosy cocoon that is familiar and keeps you safe. Being the leader of you requires the courage to step outside of that cocoon. Just as a caterpillar must break free from its comfortable cocoon to transform into a beautiful butterfly, shifting out of your comfort zone is a transformative process that allows you to spread your wings to grow and lead in alignment.

To shift outside your comfort zone first requires a decision. Deciding to do something is the critical first step because it sets the foundation for action and progress. Making a decision clarifies your intention. It helps you define what you want to achieve and creates a clear target to work towards. Without a decision you may find yourself staying inside your cocoon. Shifting outside your comfort zone requires the courage to face the unknown, take risks and challenge yourself. It involves pushing beyond the boundaries of familiarity and seeking new experiences, perspectives and opportunities.

By stepping outside your comfort zone, you cultivate resilience, adaptability and the confidence to navigate uncertainty, all of which are vital for leading yourself. The process will help you to find the elusive confidence that so many people wait to feel when they want to do something that feels like a stretch or step forward to grow.

> **HERE'S THE THING: YOU WILL NEVER JUST 'GET' CONFIDENCE.**

I also believe you'll never just be fearless. These things don't just show up. Fear, confidence and courage go hand in hand. It's about embracing fear and understanding how to tame the negative voices in your head – the ones that tell you that you can't do something or question who you are to even consider dropping that concrete ball. I'm not saying that you will be guaranteed success by doing this, nor that you will not trip and fall occasionally, but I can guarantee you that it's better to have broken free of the cocoon of your comfort zone than to stay within its confines. This process will help you to juggle the right number of balls and lead a life in alignment with your values, remain above the line and lead a life you love.

Psychologist Dr Amy Silver's book *The Loudest Guest: How to Change and Control Your Relationship with Fear* is a shining example of this. She talks about fear as the loudest guest at a dinner party. She likens it to the loudest voice in your head. If you reduce the control that fear has on you and see it as merely a guest in your mind (albeit a noisy one) and you as the host, you can dial it down to enable you to embrace courage and move forward. Dr Silver also spoke to me about the link between courage and fear on episode 85 of my podcast *Leading You*. We spoke about how you can reduce the impact of your fear to help you step into being the leader of you and to live a life you love.

Some people have trouble getting past their fear. On occasion my clients have told me their fear is paralysing or gives them panic attacks. If this is your experience, I encourage you to try a small thing first. If you want to start working with free weights at the gym, your first step might just be walking through the door and asking a staff member to show you around, so you can get familiar with where the weights are and the layout of the gym. A small step like this will give you the confidence to walk back in because you know where you are going. It will help you to break out of your comfort zone cocoon.

Join me now and decide to be the leader of your life. Write it down: 'I am the leader of me. I am [your name], the leader. I am a leader.' Now commit to it. Put your courage on like a coat. I used to see the courageous Julie as another person standing next to me. I could see her, but I couldn't *feel* her until I put her on like a coat. Until that time, I didn't move forward or take the action that I needed to. Take the work that you've already done, pick a personal goal or a professional goal and try switching your mindset to that of the leader of you. See how that could change things for you.

'I am' statements can also serve as mantras. The word 'mantra', originating from Sanskrit, combines 'man', meaning 'mind', and 'tra', meaning 'release'.[3] Consider a mantra as a meditation aid – a word or phrase you repeat. It acts as a catalyst for mind liberation, which is especially beneficial if finding focus or the right mindset proves elusive. Mantras can help us experience heightened awareness, and improved concentration and greater focus.

I use mantras daily, even when I'm not meditating. I have a ritual each morning where I will look at myself in the mirror and repeat my mantras. It definitely seemed odd at first, but there is power in looking yourself in the eye. You must believe that you can be what you are stating. For example, as I have shared with you, I believe I can be cancer-free and am doing everything in my power to remain that way. One of my mantras is 'I am living a long and healthy life cancer-free.' I believe that 100 per cent. If I didn't, there would be no point in stating it. I also say the mantra 'I am courageous, I am strong.' While I don't feel that way all the time, I believe I can be and this supports my mindset and the subsequent actions I take.

If you need help to develop your 'I am' statements or identify the characteristics you need to focus on in yourself, it's often a good idea to seek role models or use the Inspired Mindset Model in reverse to help you. The outcome you are seeking is to be the leader of you and to reflect your 'I am' statements. So, if you choose to be a courageous leader, what is the mindset that you need to adopt? It might be that stepping out of your cocoon is exciting. Then, what are the behaviours that you adopt to ensure you are walking your talk and that you embody being the courageous leader of you? It could be walking over and opening the doors to the gym for the first time, as an example. Remember, courage won't just show up. You have to take action to feel courage and confidence.

USE YOUR VOICE AND ADVOCATE FOR YOURSELF

The one thing I've learned in my life, especially throughout my cancer journey, is that you have to speak up for yourself. Imagine your voice as a key that unlocks a big red door leading to a life you love and one you are proud of. Just as this key can open the door to exciting new possibilities and opportunities, using your voice is the key to becoming the leader of you. By speaking up, expressing your thoughts and asserting your needs, you get more of what you desire and stand up for what you believe in.

You may feel vulnerable and fearful of using your voice. That is natural. It's what you decide to do with that feeling that is important. Failing to use your voice often leaves you feeling disappointed and regretful. Do this continually and you'll feel stuck and trapped. In contrast, standing up and advocating for yourself helps you to build confidence and break free of your comfort zone.

It is rare that anyone else will speak up for you – you must do this for yourself. I'm not talking about being unnaturally loud or forceful, not listening to others or not being empathetic or kind. I'm talking about saying what you need and want to say at the time that it's needed. The best way to start doing this is to be prepared, starting with the Inspired Mindset Model. Keeping the model in mind will help you in situations where you can't be prepared. Being anchored to your values, who you are and what you stand for helps with this tremendously.

Dr Brené Brown is an American professor, best-selling author of six books, podcast host and one of my most inspirational role models and mentor from afar. In her book *Daring Greatly*, Dr Brown highlights embracing vulnerability and using your voice as crucial aspects of finding courage and living wholeheartedly. She asserts that using your voice authentically and with empathy helps to build trust.

I've had to stand up and use my voice to advocate for myself often throughout my life. When I advocate for myself, it's about stressing what I want to achieve in a situation, what I want to see happen. For example, at one stage in my cancer journey I had seen seven different oncologists within a two-month period. Not only was that incredibly stressful and disruptive for me because there was no continuity of care, but each oncologist had to catch up with what I felt was a complicated history. I believed I wasn't receiving the care that I needed and I felt like I was falling through the gaps.

I spoke up – assertively. I advocated for myself to the hospital and I also spoke to my surgeon who had influence there. He supported me in my desire to see only one oncologist. Every patient is individual, every oncologist is individual. I was in a situation that was completely outside of my comfort zone and I had no experience in how to navigate it, so I needed to have some sort of certainty. At that time, I needed to secure that continuity of care for myself. If I didn't speak up, I would have had huge regrets. I'm pleased to say that from that time, I have seen the same oncologist and it's made a huge difference to how I feel and my confidence in the treatment I'm receiving.

> **USING YOUR VOICE IS IMPORTANT IN MAKING DECISIONS THAT ARE RIGHT FOR YOU AND BEING HEARD WHEN IT'S IMPORTANT, RATHER THAN LIVING WITH THE REGRET OF STAYING QUIET.**

You might be thinking, 'This is where I fall down. I have all of these dreams in my head, but I can't speak up to make them a reality.'

That might be the case, but think about what you really want. Is not speaking up what you want? Will using your voice enable you to shape a life that you love? It will get easier with practice. Start small.

In some cases it might not be culturally acceptable to speak up and doing so could lead to some severe consequences. If this is the case, do what is right for you. Hopefully reading this book has instilled some hope and given you some courage so you will be able to make the right decision and take action in time.

Right now, reflect on a situation that you're experiencing (or that you may experience in the future) where you feel hesitant in using your voice. Is it at home or at work?

A simple example that I hear often (particularly from women) is feeling afraid to ask for help in the home because their partner is too busy or their kids already have so much to do. The first step in this scenario is to think about the outcome you want. Let's say you want to ask your partner to unstack the dishwasher prior to leaving for work. The second step is to think about what you want to say. It's often helpful to explain why the desired outcome would be helpful to you, rather than diving below the line and telling the other person they are useless around the house! How can you articulate this clearly? Don't let it get to the point where you feel emotional because that might cause your words to come out in a way other than what you intended. When you're planning what to say, stay above the line. You might be feeling incredibly frustrated, but you'll get your voice across more effectively if you are above the line. The third step is to carve out the time, when you're both together and can focus on each other, to voice what you'd like. State it simply.

Regardless of what you want to say and how you want to use your voice, I encourage you to plan it out. What is your point and why is it important? How can you frame this in an assertive way, so you're not begging or pleading, but also be authentic to you? You might, for example, say something like, 'It would really help me if you could spend a couple of minutes unpacking the dishwasher in the morning so that I can get on to making the kids' lunches straight away.'

A barrier that people often face is that they worry about what other people might think if they use their voice. You can't control how others respond. I want to emphasise this because it's important.

> YOU CAN'T CONTROL OTHERS; YOU CAN ONLY CONTROL YOU.

You are the only thing that you can control in your life. You don't want to live with the regret of not saying the words that you want to say. How others respond is out of your control. All you can do is be true to yourself.

PROGRESS OVER PERFECTION

This next concept is so important to understand – not only for stepping up and using your voice, but for all of the adaptive strategies that we have discussed. 'Progress over perfection' is an often-used phrase in recovery circles. Its origin is the 12-step program of Alcoholics Anonymous. The importance of these words is that they resonate as a kind of mantra for everyone dealing with change.

Too often people focus on doing something perfectly rather than doing it anyway. It prevents many books from being released, promotions from being achieved and comfort zone cocoons from being burst. A definition of 'perfect' is having all the required or desirable elements, qualities or characteristics as good as it is possible to be; whereas progress is development or movement towards more desirable or improved conditions. Which of those two sounds more freeing?

By understanding that progress is the key to growth and leading a life you love, you'll liberate yourself from the unrealistic demands of perfectionism. I encourage you to shift your perspective from perfect to progress right now. I'm not talking about doing anything mediocre or lacking a pursuit of excellence. I'm talking about stopping the need to be perfect, because it holds you back and keeps you firmly within your comfort zone. By understanding the value of progress, you develop a deeper sense of self-acceptance and self-compassion, embracing where you're at and enabling yourself to move more freely while also welcoming the learning from any mistakes or failures along the way.

If you ensure that you stay above the line when you make a mistake, rather than berating yourself, you will learn to love mistakes as you realise they're a key part of your growth. It's important to be kind to yourself when mistakes are made. You are human, not a robot that can be programmed to do everything perfectly. This mindset shift allows you to let go of the need for external validation and the tendency to compare yourself to others. It enables you to do more of what you want and live in alignment with that. If you focus on perfection, you will never move forward.

Sheryl Sandberg's book *Lean In: Women, Work and the Will to Lead* is still one of my favourite reads about letting go of perfection and stepping outside your comfort zone. Her book is a call to arms for all women to step up and out of their comfort zone and to make decisions that are going to support them with their progress. It encourages women to lean in to what they can do as opposed to what they believe they can't. Sandberg discusses the phenomenon known as Tiara Syndrome, which refers to the tendency of many women to believe that their hard work and accomplishments alone will lead to recognition and advancement in their careers. She cites research that shows women often feel that they need to excel in every aspect of their current role before they consider themselves qualified for a promotion or a higher position. This contrasts with many men who, statistically, are more likely to pursue promotions based on their potential rather than their current achievements.

Sandberg points out that this reluctance to self-promote or seek advancement until all the boxes are checked can hold women back from taking risks and pursuing opportunities. She encourages women to challenge this mindset, to recognise their own abilities, and to be more proactive in seeking out promotions and leadership roles. The research and anecdotes Sandberg shares also highlight the need for women to be more confident, assertive and proactive in their career paths and not wait for perfect qualifications before pursuing growth opportunities.

In reading this you might be wondering if focusing on progress rather than perfection will lead to complacency or a lack of accountability. Does embracing progress mean you shouldn't strive for excellence? I'm not saying that at all – in fact, I'm saying the opposite. Excellence is different from perfection. If you focus on perfection, it will limit you. It's a never-ending quest and in pursuing it, you won't hold yourself accountable for moving forward. Striving for excellence involves pursuing high standards while maintaining a healthy and adaptive attitude towards improvement, whereas wanting perfection entails rigid, unattainable standards and a tendency to view anything less than perfect as a failure. Striving for excellence is a more balanced and sustainable approach that encourages growth, while wanting perfection can be detrimental to your wellbeing and success.

However, there are some exceptions to this. You might be in a role that does require complete precision, such as a brain surgeon or a pilot. Of course we want precision and perfection in these professions, but this does not apply to most of us.

Think back to the previous section in which we discussed asking a partner for help around the house. This is a situation in which women in particular often wait for the perfect moment to take action. But there is no such thing as a perfect moment. By having the conversation with your partner, you are making progress. Even if it doesn't go to plan, which can often happen, it doesn't mean you failed. You have progressed and there will be something to learn from it. There is also something to celebrate in it because you have made progress. It's done, it's progress.

An empowering action to take is to reflect on the growth and resilience you've cultivated through this journey of progress. Write down how you've felt along the way now that you've broken outside of your comfort zone, let go of perfection and achieved progress. You may have felt scared to have the conversation, but you are now proud of yourself. It's important to remind yourself of this as you make more progress.

When reflecting on progress versus perfection, people often think, 'I'm just not good enough. Other people will think I should've done it better.' Don't worry about other people's opinions. Others will always have an opinion. Stand firm in what you are doing and know you are good enough. You are courageous and taking steps towards leading a life you love, and that is awesome.

CONCLUSION

In this chapter, you have learned the importance of deciding to step outside of your comfort zone and be the CEO of your life. You have learned that you need to use your voice and advocate for yourself and how to dull down the voice of fear you hear when you're thinking about doing so. We've spoken about the importance of shifting your perspective from perfection to progress. Stop holding yourself back by believing that you can't be the CEO of your life. Start making decisions that will support and empower you.

Now that you have the courage to be the leader of you, in the next chapter we'll dive into actionable strategies that will propel you to new heights. We'll unlock a secret to conquering overwhelm, staying authentic, and embracing a life you truly love. It's the pivotal moment when you'll unite all the wisdom you've gained along the way.

Chapter 8

DRAWING A LINE IN THE SAND

This chapter is a critical link that will help you to avoid overwhelm. It will help you understand how to juggle the right number of balls for you, stop putting others before yourself and stick to the priorities that support you in leading a life you love. You'll see why implementing boundaries is often the missing link to achieving this, coupled with the power of a two-letter word that can have a massive impact on your life.

I've often said, 'If you don't have boundaries, you don't have standards.' I strongly believe that to be true. If you don't have boundaries in place, how can others respect you or understand how to treat you? Not having boundaries can lead to feelings of being overwhelmed, being taken advantage of or being disrespected. It's like having a house without walls that offers no protection or privacy. That would leave you feeling rather exposed! When you lack boundaries, this leaves you vulnerable to others' intrusions, expectations and demands. Just as walls provide structure and define the limits of a space, boundaries serve as the emotional and psychological barriers that safeguard your happiness and wellbeing.

In chapter 3, I demonstrated that living above the line and being curious about your life and situations as they arise is important to being the leader of you. We also explored values, which can serve as a guiding light to illuminate where your boundaries should be. Implementing the strategies that you have worked through so far is what is going to help you to adapt to change more easily, build resilience and start to do more of what you love. Implementing boundaries is key to sticking true to these strategies and not falling back into old habits.

Keep in mind that boundaries are firm but they can evolve with you. For example, you may have boundaries in place to ensure you meet your children's priorities while they are young. As they get older, these boundaries will change. Your boundaries might also need a shift during times of adjustment or change in your life's course. However, the crucial point is to have these boundaries firmly set in position. This empowers you to consciously decide when it's acceptable to allow a breach of your boundaries, while also giving you the ability to promptly reinstate them.

Boundaries can change your life. In her book *Daring Greatly*, Dr Brené Brown's research on vulnerability and shame highlights the importance of setting boundaries as an act of self-care and self-respect. She explores how boundaries help individuals establish healthy relationships, cultivate authenticity and create a life rooted in courage and wholeheartedness. According to Dr Brown, having boundaries is about finding a way to be generous towards others while continuing to lead with integrity and staying true to you. Setting boundaries means prioritising your needs and practising self-care without feeling guilty. Simply, it's knowing what's okay and what is not okay for you.

She also shares that most people aren't okay with setting boundaries because we're too worried about what other people might think. Then we become resentful and even hateful because we're doing things out of a misguided sense of obligation or that we don't want to do for the sake of pleasing others – the very definition of people pleasing. Implementing boundaries is the way to show others how to treat you. It's how you live a life true to you and one that you love.

In an article written for *Harvard Business Review*, Joe Sanok, author and TedX speaker, explains that boundaries, at their core, are all about who we give power to. He says boundaries 'force us to analyse why we may not be giving ourselves permission to work and live in the way that we feel is best for our well-being'. He points out that if we're not making decisions about our lives, schedules and workloads, who is? 'Boundaries allow us to decide when, how, and if we give this power away,' he says.[4]

He also explains that boundaries come in two types:

1. *Hard boundaries* are your non-negotiables – things you'll never compromise on, and you act on them right away. For example, I will not agree to any early morning meetings because this is when I exercise.

2. *Soft boundaries* are like goals you're more flexible about. They're things you want, but you're open to compromise. For instance, aiming to leave work at 4.30pm instead of 5.30pm is a soft boundary. It's a goal to finish by 4.30, but you're okay with leaving a little later if circumstances get in the way.

Identifying boundaries as 'hard' or 'soft' helps you distinguish what you won't budge on versus your more flexible goals. It empowers you to make choices aligned with your core needs and manage your energy as you work towards the rest.

I can assure you that maintaining boundaries is something I've had to work on, but I'm certainly grateful for having them – particularly when I was diagnosed with melanoma, and also while writing this book. My boundaries have had to be hard to ensure I achieve the deadlines for the book and that I can look after my health in the best way possible. So I'm excited to explore this with you so you can experience the immense benefits too. It's a life changer!

THE SECRET TO CHANGE

Maddy is a senior corporate leader renowned for her exceptional abilities. Others have always heavily relied upon her to lead large, complex projects to success. She has constantly received accolades for her work. She has also constantly received feedback that she looks tired. Amid her accomplishments, a hidden struggle persisted – her willingness to let others syphon her energy. The constant giving left her drained and weary, a far cry from the vibrant leader she felt she once was.

Maddy recognised the need for change and reached out to me for coaching. Her problem was that she didn't have boundaries in place to protect her energy. Every ounce she had, she gave to others. She allowed too many people to zap her energy, receiving nothing in return.

She made a decision that would change her life. She implemented a hard boundary, a shield to safeguard her energy and wellbeing.

Maddy determined with absolute clarity what this boundary looked and felt like and what she would now say no to. She felt liberated.

No longer could others indiscriminately tap into her reserves. She progressively educated people about how to communicate with her, and resisted the urge to fall back into old habits. Instead, Maddy's energy flourished. She gradually returned to the woman she was – vibrant and invigorated.

> **BOUNDARIES ARE THE SECRET TO CHANGE, YET THEY'RE SOMETHING PEOPLE OFTEN FEEL GUILTY FOR HAVING.**

Implementing boundaries will support you in juggling the right number of balls for you and doing what is in alignment with how you want to live. You'll be able to make an empowered choice about whether you will juggle another ball for a short time if you're asked to, or have the confidence to be able to say no. Boundaries will help you to stop falling into the people-pleaser trap and instead say the magic word: no.

Boundaries offer you the ability to:

- build strong self-esteem and self-respect
- build strong relationships and partnerships that are equal
- protect your energy and emotional wellbeing
- gradually share information about yourself as appropriate (avoiding the 'overshare')
- advocate for yourself and to be compassionately assertive by confidently saying yes or no

- value your needs and priorities rather than being influenced by others.

Maddy's story is not unique. Boundaries are something that I see many people lacking – those I've worked with, my coaching clients, and friends and family members. When there are no clear boundaries in place, bad habits flourish and you slowly start to live life on others' terms.

> **I LIKEN BOUNDARIES TO DRAWING A LINE IN THE SAND. KNOWING WHERE YOUR BOUNDARIES ARE MEANS UNDERSTANDING WHERE THE LINE IS – WHAT IS ACCEPTABLE AND WHAT IS UNACCEPTABLE TO YOU IN VARIOUS ASPECTS OF YOUR LIFE.**

By defining your boundaries, you establish a framework that enables you to make choices aligned with your values and priorities. Boundaries provide you with clarity, allowing you to invest your time and energy in areas that truly matter. They create the space for personal growth, self-care and doing what is in line with your priorities.

The Stop, Start framework shown in figure 4 is something I introduced in my book *Busy*. It's an awesome framework that can be used to assess where you need to implement boundaries. You can identify what you need to stop doing and what you want to start doing, and develop your boundaries accordingly. In Maddy's case, she wanted to *stop* freely giving her energy away and allowing others to zap it from her. She wanted to *start* protecting her energy and educating people on how to communicate with her.

Figure 4: Stop, Start framework

Many people I coach have a goal of getting more and better-quality sleep. Lack of quality sleep is definitely a problem in our society, as shown by a Deloitte Access Economics health report indicating that 39.8 per cent of Australians don't get enough sleep and it's costing our economy billions.[5] To achieve a goal of getting more and better-quality sleep you need to establish a consistent bedtime routine and have boundaries in place to achieve this. These might include:

- *Set a specific time to go to bed each night:* Allow yourself enough hours for a restful sleep.
- *Create a technology curfew:* Avoid using electronic devices, such as smartphones or laptops, for at least one hour before bedtime.
- *Designate a calm sleep environment:* Keep your bedroom clutter-free, dark, and at a comfortable temperature to promote quality sleep.

- *Limit caffeine intake:* Avoid consuming caffeinated beverages or foods, especially in the evening, as they can interfere with sleep.
- *Communicate your sleep schedule:* Inform your family members, roommates or partner about your sleep goals, requesting their support in maintaining a quiet environment during your designated sleep hours.
- *Say no to late-night commitments:* Refrain from taking on additional responsibilities or social engagements that will keep you up past your bedtime.
- *Prioritise self-care:* Allocate time for relaxation activities, such as reading a book, taking a bath or practising mindfulness, before sleep.
- *Avoid excessive napping:* Limit daytime napping to short power naps, preferably earlier in the day, to prevent them from interfering with your night-time sleep.
- *Set boundaries with work:* Establish clear limits with work-related tasks. Avoid bringing work into your bedroom and ensure you have adequate time to unwind before bed.
- *Practise assertive communication:* Learn to express your sleep needs assertively to others, advocating for yourself and ensuring others respect your boundaries.

If sleep is a priority for you, you need to make it happen and ensure you have boundaries in place to facilitate it.

> SELF-RESPECT IS AT THE VERY HEART OF THIS. HAVING A HEALTHY LEVEL OF RESPECT FOR YOURSELF ENABLES YOU TO LIVE LIFE ON YOUR TERMS, RATHER THAN WHAT OTHERS DICTATE.

If you don't have boundaries in place, you can become a slave to technology and lose track of precious time. This is a common pitfall. Our work now transcends the office door and permeates our entire lives. We are totally accessible via our smartphones. Many people I speak with tell me they are 'too busy' to exercise, to eat well, to pause for self-reflection. However, when I ask them to measure the amount of time they spend on their phones, looking at emails or social platforms as an example, the time wasted is astounding. They could have fit in seven 30-minute walks and prepared seven healthy meals in the time they wasted mindlessly scrolling. They were simply unaware how much time was being lost to something that wasn't supporting their life other than being a distraction. This is something I suggest you do also – measure the amount of time you spend scrolling through social media. This is a massive time zapper and something that needs firm boundaries around if you are going to look after yourself and lead a life you love.

I'm not advocating for having boundaries in place that are hard and rigid, and can't be changed if needed. These will limit your growth. Having boundaries in place that are too strong can foster ignorance – for example, using a personal boundary as a reason to avoid listening to another opinion. There needs to be a balance when you're creating boundaries to ensure you are open to change, rather than remaining stuck in your ways or remaining in your comfort zone.

There may be situations where you need to compromise your boundaries. For example, someone close to you might unexpectedly need you in an emergency, which will cross a boundary that you've put in place to protect your personal time or your bedtime routine. If this is the case, be flexible while knowing it's a decision that is in line with who you are and your values, and that it's a one-off. When you've made a habit out of sticking to your boundaries, it's so much easier to get back on the horse after allowing one to be crossed!

I encourage you to now push the pause button and take some time for self-reflection. Using the Stop, Start framework I shared with you, identify an area in your life where you feel your boundaries are being tested or compromised. You might be feeling frustrated or let down, for example. What can you stop and start doing to shore up your boundaries around this situation? You could also reflect on how many balls you are juggling, and which balls you need to stop and start to juggle.

Once you've identified these areas, make a list of your non-negotiable or hard boundaries. What or who do you need to say no to? If you are saying yes to things that are compromising your boundaries, explore why you are saying yes. Is it fear? Is it the need to please? Do you want to feel needed, for example?

You can also use the Inspired Mindset Model to help you work out the outcome that you are seeking. Use 'I' statements – 'I will go to bed at 9.00pm. I will keep my phone in another room. I will say no when...' Practise reinforcing these priorities and observe the impact on your overall wellbeing and relationships.

You might struggle to do this because you fear people will reject you if you say no to their requests. This is totally normal and understandable. It may not feel good at first. Remember, you are creating change here and stepping outside of your comfort zone. It will feel different. Stick with it and it will get easier. Practise is progress.

THE POWER OF NO

Contrary to popular belief, you can't do everything all at once, nor can you effectively juggle too many crystal balls at any one time. Eventually, you will tire and one will smash. You can't say yes to everything. Given how many requests you probably field every day, you'll need to say no to some or even many requests. The word no is your superpower, maintaining the boundaries that you put in place.

Naomi Simson, CEO and founder of RedBalloon, is an entrepreneur, author, speaker and was a 'shark' (investor) on the TV show *Shark Tank*. At an event I saw her speak at, she shared how no is a full statement for her. She gave us permission to say the word no without having to follow it with a justification or an excuse. At first, I thought, 'Whoa, that is tough. Imagine just saying no to someone. I've often wanted to say it but never have.' You might also be thinking the same: 'I could never say that.' But trust me, you can.

Setting boundaries can often feel uncomfortable at first. You may find that people will push back when you start saying no or assertively communicating your needs. They may not be clear on why you are behaving in a different way than what they are used to experiencing from you. They may try to test your limits, to see how serious you are about drawing the line. That doesn't mean that you're doing something wrong. It just highlights that you need to be clear and consistent until people adjust to the new way of interacting. This is where saying no becomes your superpower.

I understand that saying no can be incredibly hard to do – especially for the people pleasers of the world, of which there are many. I am happy to say I am a recovering people pleaser. It was a very old habit of mine that didn't serve me at all. Any change can evoke feelings of anxiety or discomfort – especially when you are changing the way you interact with people or changing an ingrained habit that you have held onto for a long time. Saying no can be particularly difficult for people who need to feel needed. I find this is often the case with women, but it's definitely not gender specific. Nor is it something to be ashamed of – rather, it's something to be aware of.

There is a common fear that saying a flat-out no will upset people, cause them not to like you or cause them not to need you in the future. I totally get it and have been there too. It's okay to say, 'I'm sorry, I can't do that tonight.' That is a kinder way of saying no. But you will notice that it's not followed by a justification or an excuse. It's a bit less abrasive than simply saying no, though, and enables you to stand firm in your decision.

Paulo Coelho has a wonderful saying: 'When you say yes to others, make sure you are not saying no to yourself.' This is such a great reminder to check in with yourself and ensure you are living in alignment with your goals.

Knowing where your boundaries are and how you want to live your life allows you to say a positive no at the right time for the right reasons.

> IF YOU WANT TO LEAD A LIFE YOU LOVE,
> YOU SIMPLY MUST LEARN TO SAY NO.

It allows you to say yes to more of what you love and protects your time and energy. By using this powerful word wisely, you cultivate self-respect, build stronger boundaries and foster healthier relationships.

Social psychologist Dr Vanessa K Bohns said, 'Many people agree to do things, even things they would prefer not to do, simply to avoid the considerable discomfort of saying no.'[6] Her research reveals that setting boundaries and saying no can lead to increased feelings of empowerment, improved self-esteem and better work-life balance.

A very common question that I am asked while delivering workshops and keynotes is, 'How do I say no to my boss, when doing so would be considered inappropriate?' I agree with this sentiment and I certainly understand that saying no directly may not be a good career decision! You might consider saying something like, 'I'd be happy to do that, but I have many other competing priorities. Can we work out what needs to be done first?' In doing so you are communicating clearly and with clarity; it's a really positive way to say no to your boss (and others, for that matter).

There are numerous approaches to saying no in an assertive way. Perhaps try doing this with someone you know well first, who loves and respects you. See how it feels. Remember, practise is progress. The more you say no and stick to your boundaries, the easier it will be. Harnessing the power of no and embracing boundaries is about creating a life that reflects your values, protects your wellbeing and leads to more joy. Using this powerful word wisely empowers you to live a life you genuinely love.

One of the keys to saying no is increasing your self-awareness about why you say yes! Think about how many concrete balls you were juggling when you started reading this book, or reflect on a recent situation where you have said a reluctant yes and wished afterwards that you had said no. What was the reason you said yes? Was it out of a fear of disappointing others? A fear of rejection? A need to be needed? Because you wanted to please? Write this down. You might like to use the Stop, Start framework to gain more clarity. Remember, you are not berating yourself, simply becoming more aware.

Thinking of this situation, how would saying no have supported you to live a life you love? How could you have said no without a convoluted justification? Write down ways that you could say no in a similar situation that might arise. Practise saying these words out loud and anchor yourself to why it would have served you better to say no. Believe me, this works. Practise is progress.

Your next step is to say no when you know that no is the right response.

CONCLUSION

In this chapter, you've learned about the importance of setting boundaries and the power of saying no. This is your link to juggling the right number of balls for you at any given time and leading a life you love. This is not only empowering, but liberating. It's about living your life on your terms and creating a legacy that you are proud of. Know that I am doing this process every single day, so I am walking right beside you.

Stop living your life through a misguided sense of obligation or in a way that suits others. Start living your life on your terms and set boundaries to support you, your energy and your happiness.

In the next chapter, I'll show you how to measure your success and to further define the life you want. We'll also explore an important step that many people forget to do when implementing change: celebrating your success. This is where we're going to have fun.

Chapter 9

SUCCESS ON YOUR TERMS

Success is different for everyone. You might want to transform your entire life, or simply stop eating Tim Tams. The important thing is you must know your measure of success and *why* it matters to you. This might seem obvious, but I can assure you, through the knowledge gained by years of coaching and my own experience, it's not.

Often people lack clarity about what they want to achieve. No doubt you want to be successful, but what does that mean for you? Why do you want it? If you want to put yourself forward for a promotion or start training for a triathlon, what is your compelling reason to do so? Understanding the *why* is a key factor in determining success on your terms.

Success is often portrayed as a fixed destination, but on your terms it's more about the journey itself. It's about setting goals and milestones that align with your vision for the life you love. This means crafting a career, relationships and lifestyle that reflect your individual definition of success, rather than conforming to external standards or success that's defined by comparison.

When you're unclear or have no definition of what success looks like, you are constantly striving to reach an unknown destination. This can be exhausting and deflating, and may cause you to become a victim of comparison.

In a world driven by social media highlight reels and societal standards, it's tempting to measure our worth based on others' achievements and appearances.

> **FALLING INTO THE COMPARISON TRAP BREEDS DISSATISFACTION AND ROBS YOU OF THE JOY OF YOUR OWN ACCOMPLISHMENTS.**

Instead, focus on your individual progress. Set personal goals aligned with your values and celebrate every step forward, irrespective of others' journeys. This shift in mindset leads to improved mental wellbeing, increased self-esteem and deeper satisfaction. This is about designing a life you love, not a life that you *think* you'll love or that others will love for you.

Something we often forget to do is celebrate our success – not only when we reach our goals but the milestones along the way. Celebrating success means recognising and acknowledging the milestones you achieve, no matter how small, and taking the time to reward yourself for your progress. So many of my clients are prone to simply ticking off a goal list and then focusing on what's next. There's no popping of a champagne cork or even a moment taken to acknowledge their effort.

Celebrating your success is an important strategy in building confidence and increasing your motivation to stick with your goals.

It's so important to do, but often neglected when we get caught up in the busyness of life. By defining your success and celebrating reaching your milestones, you build confidence and are less likely to fall into the comparison trap. This is your key to owning and creating the life that you love.

In this chapter, we're going to explore success on your terms, leading you to a life that you love; the importance of creating milestones along the way that can be celebrated; and how to avoid the comparison trap. We'll also go deeper into celebrating success, which is my favourite part of this chapter and something we don't do often enough as high-achieving people.

DEFINING YOUR SUCCESS

After many years of asking others what success means to them and getting vague responses, I've developed a theory about why people are unclear about this. When I enter into any contract with a client – whether it be a keynote, a coaching relationship or a workshop – I always ask the question, 'When we've completed this project, what will success look like to you?' A common thread that I've identified through their responses is that people want to *feel* differently in some way. It's not always about a material goal; it transcends the obvious, and that's why people often can't pinpoint it. When we get to the heart of it, they might want to feel less overwhelmed, more motivated, more connected to their values or happier.

Then, as we discussed earlier, it's about understanding why you want to achieve the goal. Why does it matter? Is this something that goes beyond an egocentric goal, or does it have deep meaning to you?

> **KNOWING YOUR MEASURE OF SUCCESS IS ABOUT EXPANDING YOUR SELF-AWARENESS AND DEEPENING YOUR UNDERSTANDING OF WHO YOU ARE AND WHAT BRINGS YOU GENUINE HAPPINESS AND FULFILMENT.**

It requires pressing the pause button to reflect on your passions, strengths and core values.

Your measure of success will be different to mine. I might be happy reading a book a year; you might be happy reading a book a week. But defining your success goes deeper than simply reading a book. So you read a book a week – mind you, if you can do that, I applaud you – but what do you get out of reading that book? Is it something to brag about or is it important for your growth? Does it expand your knowledge or self-awareness? Does it challenge your thinking? Does it transport you away for an hour of relaxation every day?

Too often you'll hear celebrities who have fame and fortune speak about how unhappy they are, even though becoming rich and famous was their ultimate goal. Be careful what you wish for. Ensuring your goals are meaningful and purposeful to you, and only you, is important. Looking for external validation as a sign of success is fraught with danger. You are handing your power over to others and determining your success by what others think.

Theodore Roosevelt once said, 'Comparison is the thief of joy.' I believe this to be true. In a world driven by social media we have 24/7 access into the lives of others, many with better bodies, more money, more happiness, more fun and more adventure than us – or so it seems. Our inclination to compare ourselves to others has a biological basis: our brain seeks to gauge our worth in relation to others. But this can take us off track, deplete our confidence and hijack our progress.

Comparison plays a fundamental role in shaping our self-perception and understanding of our strengths and weaknesses, as explained by London Business School's Professor Thomas Mussweiler, an expert in organisational behaviour. This mental calculation often occurs unconsciously and rapidly. You have no idea that you're doing it. This is often referred to as social comparison.

Clinical psychologist Dr Joyce Chong says that social comparison involves evaluating ourselves in relation to others, spanning areas like work, academics, wealth, popularity, sports, and appearance.[7] Two types of comparisons are significant: upward and downward comparisons. Upward comparisons are when you measure yourself against those you consider superior in a given domain, such as star employees, top students, the most popular individuals or social media 'influencers'. Conversely, downward comparisons involve gauging yourself against those you perceive as performing worse in a particular area or who are not as successful as you believe you are. Research indicates that people with lower self-esteem tend to make more upward comparisons, but this often leads to decreased self-worth, forming a counterproductive cycle.[8]

Upward comparisons manifest in various contexts:

- *Work:* Comparing yourself unfavourably to a colleague who was awarded leadership of a project, assuming their superior competence.
- *Sports:* Feeling inferior while comparing your slower progress in training to another's exceptional progress, even though they have less experience.

- *Family:* Pitting yourself against others whose children behave better in public, evoking feelings of inadequacy.
- *Self-image:* Evaluating a photograph of someone you see on social media looking great and feeling self-conscious about your own appearance in comparison.

However, some use upward comparison to motivate self-improvement – for example, someone aspiring to run faster emulating the techniques of an accomplished runner. To benefit from using upward comparisons you need to be aware of what works for you and what doesn't.

While our innate need for connection and belonging drives us to compare, continuous comparison jeopardises your wellbeing and mental health. It is essential to recognise the potential toxicity of excessive comparison and the risks it poses to your happiness. Instead, being kind to yourself and focusing on self-acceptance, gratitude and your own success journey can lead to a healthier and more fulfilling mindset.

Please remember: the social media world is curated according to what people want you to see. It's not reality. I strongly encourage you to understand whether social media is serving you or depleting you – and if it's the latter, avoid it or unfollow people who make you feel that way.

> UNDERSTANDING AND AVOIDING THE COMPARISON TRAP CAN LEAD TO PROFOUND SELF-ACCEPTANCE AND GENUINE HAPPINESS.

You'll experience reduced stress and anxiety as you release the burden of constantly 'measuring up'.

Defining success on your terms empowers you to escape the pressure of external expectations. You'll experience increased self-confidence and a greater sense of purpose, as you're living a life in alignment and one you love. Moreover, it fosters resilience, as your motivation stems from within, enabling you to navigate challenges with greater determination.

Embarking on defining your success can sometimes feel overwhelming. You might think, 'Where do I start?' or 'How do I think beyond the obvious – career and finances?' Coming up, I will show you a great exercise to help you. By taking this action you'll be avoiding the comparison trap and be focused on what matters to you, and what is in line with your values and vision for a life that you love.

When I was recovering from my surgery, I had to redefine what success looked like for me. I created little milestones to rebuild my confidence and keep my focus on my journey, not on what I was missing out on. This activity helped me a lot.

You might think this is pointless and irrelevant because change is constant, therefore why have goals? Good point: change is constant and anything we do, including setting goals, requires an element of flexibility. Your success will evolve and change as your life continues to evolve. You need to be flexible enough to be able to respond to change and adjust your definitions of success accordingly.

An awesome place to start is to look at your life holistically using a tool called the Wheel of Life. You might've heard of this before. The original concept was developed by Paul J Meyer in the 1960s to help people achieve their goals. Looking at figure 5, rate all areas of your life on a scale of one to ten. Once you've done this activity, you'll get a clear picture of what needs attention. You'll be able to establish goals to address the areas you would like to improve or even leverage. The choice is yours – but it must mean something to you.

When I'm setting goals I will generally do so using two columns. I'll list the goal, as well as why I want to achieve it. In the past, I used to write down goals that sounded good or that I thought I *should* do as part of my profession, but when I asked myself why the goal mattered, my response was very ego driven. It wasn't a meaningful goal for me – I wanted to look good in others' eyes. That's no reason to establish a goal!

Figure 5: The Wheel of Life

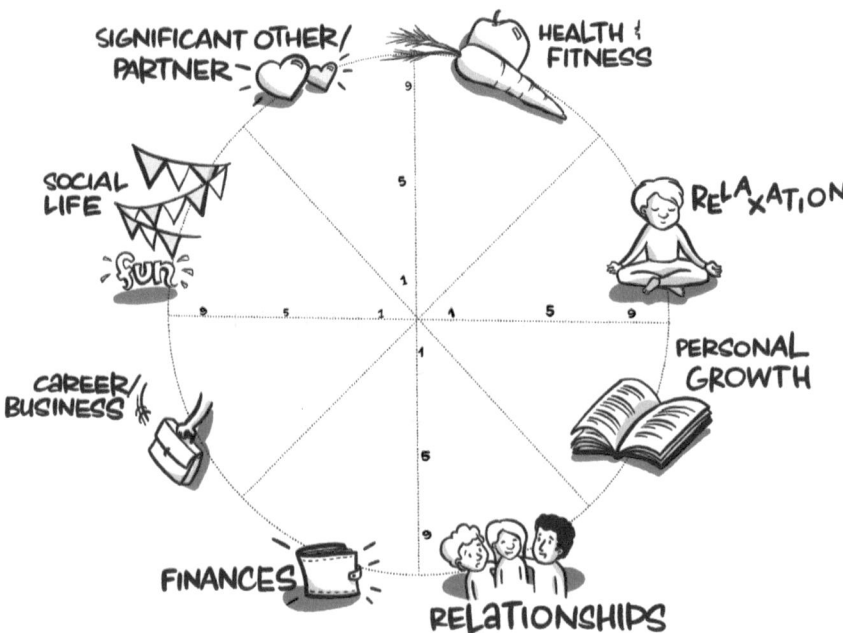

Once you have defined your goals you can then identify the milestones and achievements that matter most as part of each goal. This process helps to align your actions with your values and aspirations.

I recommend starting with four key areas with three goals in each. Define what success looks like for you in each area. Let's say one area is fun. Your goal might be to see one movie a month, or to laugh every day. I do this quarterly so my goals aren't too big, they look achievable and I have 12 things I can celebrate each quarter.

You might feel anxious about setting goals. You might be scared that you'll fail and don't want to put yourself into this situation. I understand this, and it's common. Try this exercise with a friend. Focus on just one area and ask your friend to support you or even decide on one together for fun. See how you go with it.

CELEBRATING MOMENTS

In 2006, I backpacked around China with a friend. Towards the end of our trip, we climbed part of the beautiful Yellow Mountains. It is a World Heritage site and has spectacular scenery. We were lucky: it was a beautiful, warm day. It was hard yakka because it was a really steep climb. I have a tendency to want to get a physical challenge done quickly, but I physically couldn't due to its scale and the amount of people on the path. We had to stop along the way, and doing so was incredibly worthwhile. The views were glorious. The air was so fresh. Every stop we made gave us another sensory delight. If I had just kept my head down in determination and kept going, I would have missed out on some spectacular and beautiful memories. My lesson in that was to be present more – to celebrate the little moments on the path to the peak where the goal is.

Too often we can strive our way forward, tick off our goals and think about what's next without celebrating the moment and what we've already achieved. When I reflect on climbing the mountain in China, I apply the same principle to my cancer journey. I still have a huge component of that mountain to climb and sometimes I get knocked down. But celebrating my little moments – like a great scan result, good blood test result, increasing exercise, being able to concentrate for longer or feeling less fatigued – helps me to face my challenges. Celebrating the small wins stimulates the release of dopamine – a feel-good brain chemical that reinforces the learning experience and strengthens our connection to our goals.

It's so important to celebrate your successes – big and small – along the way and upon achievement, and not simply focus on what's next. This builds your confidence and motivation and allows you to have fun too. Celebrating success means acknowledging and rewarding yourself for the progress you make towards your goals. It means taking time to reflect on your accomplishments, no matter how small, and appreciating the effort and dedication you have invested.

> BY CELEBRATING THESE MILESTONES, YOU INCREASE MOTIVATION AND BOOST SELF-CONFIDENCE, WHICH FUELS CONTINUED PROGRESS.

At a deeper level, celebrating the small moments along the way enables you to be more present, have gratitude for your progress and hopefully have some fun.

You might have heard of the phrase, 'Success breeds success.' More specifically, 'The more you experience success, the more likely you are to succeed.' In a study by Stony Brook University, researchers used website-based experiments to uncover whether 'success breeds success' is a reality.[9] Researchers found that early success bestowed on individuals produced significant increases in subsequent rates of success. Therefore, creating smaller milestones as part of your bigger goal and allowing yourself to feel a sense of success more often will increase your success in achieving your bigger goal.

Our journey through this book has been extensive, and this chapter brings together all that we have traversed collectively. Your success is your own. Own it and celebrate it. In every single chapter you've bravely confronted or explored a certain area of your life that may have challenged your thinking or reminded you of habits you wish to break. That in itself is an achievement. Celebrate it. Do something that lights you up. Your celebrations don't have to be something huge. Take yourself for a coffee with a friend on a beautiful day. Have a glass of bubbles with your partner. Take yourself off to a movie you want to see. Put on your favourite music and dance up a storm. Buy yourself a lovely bunch of flowers. Do anything, as long as it's meaningful for you.

Videographer and podcast host Rebecca Saunders does this really well. She has a bottle of champagne in the fridge labelled with a goal that she wants to achieve that will help her with her ultimate goal. Every time she achieves a goal, out comes the champagne and pop goes the cork. She celebrates every moment and it motivates her to continue.

When I achieve smaller goals, I love to buy myself a gorgeous bunch of flowers or head to the beach and take some time out. When I conquer a large goal, I'll celebrate with my husband with dinner at a favourite restaurant. These are things I love to do.

You might be thinking, 'If I celebrate success along the way, I'll get complacent. It feeds my appetite for success too much rather than keeping me hungry for it.' You know you and how you're wired, but I don't believe in starving ourselves of success in order to reach a pinnacle. We need to nourish ourselves along the way. In a highly competitive environment where constant progress is expected, celebrating every small achievement may not be practical or aligned with the prevailing culture. If this is the case, be a disruptor and try it on for yourself anyway. You never know, it might make you even more successful – which may inspire cultural change.

What should you do now? Here are some ideas:

- Start with a weekly ritual of pressing the pause button at a certain time of the week – perhaps on a Friday afternoon. It's an excellent way to end the week.
- Reflect on your achievements, big and small, and write them down. Perhaps on one day an achievement might be simply getting out of bed, or making the bed. Write it down each and every day – regardless of how small you think it was, you will have achieved something.
- Take a moment to acknowledge yourself. You might high five yourself or give yourself a gold star. Whatever works.
- Treat yourself to a meaningful reward or engage in a self-care activity that brings you joy and rejuvenation. Is it a piece of your favourite cake with a lovely pot of tea, a wine and cheese platter with your partner or eating chocolate strawberries in the bath? I might be giving away my reward ideas here that mostly revolve around food, but you get the idea.
- Notice how you feel when you're experiencing your reward. Remember to be present in the moment.
- Write down your achievements, big and small, and you'll feel better. Often, we need to remind ourselves of how fabulous we are. This is also an awesome strategy to refer to when you're having moments of self-doubt or feeling less confident than you'd like.

You might be resisting this because you're thinking, 'I don't have the money to be constantly celebrating.' Monetary rewards are not always needed. Simply ringing a bell, similar to what cancer patients do when they finish a round of chemo, or jumping up and down on the spot can work too, as can sharing your success with a friend. Verbalising your achievement and why it's so important to you can often be more meaningful than anything requiring money.

CONCLUSION

In this chapter you've learned the importance of determining your own success and avoiding the comparison trap. You understand that your goals or definition of success must mean something to you and that you need to stop and celebrate your milestones along the way. You also now understand how this fuels your confidence and gives you the incentive to keep on going when life gets tough.

Have fun with this. Put on your party shoes and celebrate you. You deserve it. Stop comparing yourself to others or striving for success you think others expect of you. Start owning your success and create a life that you love.

Now you know everything that I know. You're empowered to make a choice to lead a life you love. You have lots of strategies and tools that will encourage you to be the leader of your life. It's over to you.

CONCLUSION

Dear Leaders,

You now possess an extraordinary power – the power of choice. It is within your control to shape your life, regardless of the challenges that come your way. Your response to life's events is your choice. With all of the knowledge you've explored in this book, you can navigate any obstacle with confidence, resilience and a solution-focused mindset.

> CHANGE IS AN OPPORTUNITY FOR GROWTH AND YOU HOLD THE KEY TO ADAPT AND LEAD YOUR WAY THROUGH IT ALL. YOUR LIFE IS YOURS TO LOVE.

I've learned this truth through my own transformative cancer journey. Rather than letting it control or define me, I chose to rise above it. Now I share my story with you in the hope that it will inspire you to do two things: take control of your life, and take melanoma seriously and prioritise your health. Your health is invaluable, a precious gift that deserves your utmost care. Take the time to get your skin checked along with every other form of self-care, such as bowel and breast checks – a simple yet essential step towards ensuring your long-term vitality. By getting your skin checked, you can detect any potential risks early on, potentially saving your life. By embracing a proactive approach to your health, you not only guard your own wellbeing, but also set an example for others to follow. If my words can make a difference in even one person's life, then writing this book was worth every effort.

Imagine if everyone in the world followed the principles that you have explored and adopted in this book. Imagine people taking responsibility for their actions, leading themselves through their life, being able to dig into their resilience for the tough times. Imagine if people could be confident in who they are, but self-aware enough to respect and be curious about other cultures, religions, gender identities and ways of living. Imagine if people were loving their life. The world would be a much better place for it.

When you lead yourself through your life, you step up into a different zone. You are a role model for others and inspire them to do the same. When others see you being courageous, confident and stepping outside of your comfort zone, even when feeling vulnerable, they're inspired to step up too. This is how movements are created and strong legacies are built.

The power of choice brings challenges, especially when choosing to lead with integrity and rise above negativity. As Michelle Obama famously stated during the 2016 Democratic National Convention, 'When they go low, we go high.' This embodies the essence of being a leader who constantly chooses to lead above the line.

Anchoring yourself to your values and maintaining boundaries may alter your interactions with others. Some may struggle with this shift, making you feel guilty or doubt yourself.

CONCLUSION

> **BUT REMEMBER, STAYING TRUE TO WHO YOU ARE IS THE ULTIMATE TEST OF LEADERSHIP.**

Stick to what you now know. Remind yourself that it is not what happens to you but how you respond that truly matters. This is a true test of a leader.

Join me and my tribe of leaders and changemakers, united in our mission to create a brighter world. Together we recognise the profound impact of our actions, knowing that the ripple effects of change we create in our own spheres extend far beyond what we can imagine. By embracing our power to make a difference, we inspire others to do the same and make the world a better place.

One of my greatest joys and achievements is to see my clients shine – to step up and into the person they always were, lead a life they love and create a legacy that they are proud of. That is what I want for you also. The best part is, I'm confident you can do it. I'm cheering you on all the way.

Wishing you only the best,

Julie x

ABOUT THE AUTHOR

Here's a little confession: I've got a serious soft spot for '80s glam rock. My all-time favourite band? Def Leppard. And when they roll into Australia for a concert, you can bet I'm front and centre, living it up like it's the '80s.

But hold on, don't be fooled into thinking I'm stuck in the past – well, except when it comes to my music taste!

In my professional world, I'm a game-changer. I empower my clients with expert strategies, self-awareness and the wisdom I've earned through my own life experiences. As a coach, speaker and author, I'm on a mission to show leaders how to shake things up in an ever-changing world and achieve extraordinary results.

However, 2021 served me a card I couldn't exchange – cancer. Let's not sugar-coat it; it's been no walk in the park. But here's the twist: I see the diagnosis itself as a game-changer. It's taught me a lesson – in life and leadership, you've got to lead yourself first and embrace the joy in every moment.

In an age where overwhelm is often the norm, smart and savvy individuals are seeking to master the art of juggling, embrace change, and truly savour the life they lead – not just endure it.

This is where I come into play.

With experience managing teams of 130 in the corporate world before launching my own business back in 2007, I've got the whole picture. I've transformed big businesses from toxic to top-notch. The best of the lot raked in over $20 million in profit. I've collaborated with leaders to boost team sales by a staggering 200 per cent and triple the size of their businesses. I've revived lagging leaders, the ones in the 'bottom third', turning them into star performers and role models who change the game.

In simple terms, I know what it takes to excel at what you do. I know what it takes to be the game-changer. To step inside, leaving the hustle and bustle at the door, and start a fresh game – one that brings you pure happiness.

If you're as passionate as I am about changing the game in this ever-evolving world and becoming an inspiring, fearless role model, reach out and let's connect. Together, we can rock the stage of life!

juliehyde.com.au

ACKNOWLEDGEMENTS

First and foremost, I owe an immeasurable debt of gratitude to my husband, Craig. He's not just my life partner; he's the unwavering pillar of support that enables me to be me and pour my heart and soul into my work. 'Thank you' hardly begins to convey my appreciation.

Kath Walters, my book coach and wise counsel, is an absolute gem. When I found you, I struck gold. Your program, your guidance, your support and your honest feedback were instrumental in shaping this book. You challenged my thinking and managed to extract the ideas from my head and heart, pushing me to do my very best. Joining forces with you was unquestionably one of the best decisions I've made.

To the incredible team at Publish Central, particularly Michael and Anna, I extend my heartfelt gratitude. You helped me turn my dream into reality and made the entire process seamless. Your teamwork is nothing short of amazing.

My editor, Brooke Lyons, is not just an editing wizard; she's a beautiful soul. She worked her magic on my words, ensuring they shone brilliantly. Working with you was a pleasure, and your guidance was invaluable.

To my support team and first readers – Catherine, Michelle, Mel and Carlo – I can't thank you enough. Your unwavering support, encouragement and considered feedback played an essential role in making *You Always Have a Choice* the best it could be. I'm not only blessed to have you on my team but also to have your friendship.

My dear friends, thank you for your patience and understanding. Your belief in me, coupled with your unwavering support, has been a source of inspiration and strength on my journey. Your friendship and encouragement are deeply cherished.

Lastly, to you, dear reader, this book is dedicated. Your pursuit of a life you love and the joy you experience mean the world to me. I'm profoundly grateful that you invested your time in reading this book, and I hope it brings you the inspiration and guidance you seek on your path to a life filled with happiness. Thank you for being a part of this journey.

REFERENCES

1. Giada Di Stefano et al. (2023), 'Learning by Thinking: How Reflection Can Spur Progress Along the Learning Curve', Harvard Business School NOM Unit Working Paper No. 14-093, Kenan Institute of Private Enterprise Research Paper No. 2414478.

2. Mia Primeau (2021), 'Your powerful, changeable mindset', *Stanford Report*, accessed 4 October 2023. https://news.stanford.edu/report/2021/09/15/mindsets-clearing-lens-life/

3. Crystal Raypole (2020), 'Have Trouble Meditating? Try Mantra Meditation', *Healthline*, accessed 6 October 2023. https://www.healthline.com/health/mantra-meditation

4. Joe Sanok (2022), 'A Guide to Setting Better Boundaries', *Harvard Business Review*, accessed 19 October 2023. https://hbr.org/2022/04/a-guide-to-setting-better-boundaries

5. Deloitte Access Economics and Sleep Health Foundation (2017), 'Asleep on the job: Costs of inadequate sleep in Australia', accessed 8 October 2023. https://www.sleephealthfoundation.org.au/special-sleep-reports/asleep-on-the-job-costs-of-inadequate-sleep-in-australia

6 Vanessa K Bohns (2016), '(Mis)Understanding Our Influence Over Others: A Review of the Underestimation-of-Compliance Effect', *Current Directions in Psychological Science*, 25:119–123.

7 Joyce Chong (2022), 'Low self-esteem: the role of social comparison', *The Skill Collective*, accessed 8 October 2023. https://theskillcollective.com/blog/low-self-esteem-social-comparison

8 JV Wood, SE Taylor and RR Lichtman (1985), 'Social comparison in adjustment to breast cancer', *Journal of Personality and Social Psychology*, 49(5): 1169–1183.

9 Stony Brook University (2014), 'Success breeds success, study confirms', *Science Daily*, accessed 19 October 2023. https://www.sciencedaily.com/releases/2014/04/140428154838.htm

'Julie is one of the most authentic leadership coaches and mentors I have come across. Through her own lived experiences, she is so well equipped to lead others on their journey of self. She illuminates the path to personal empowerment and transformation, reminding us that the power of choice is the key to a better tomorrow.'

– Gill Ragus, Regional Sales Manager

'My experience with executive coaching has been invaluable. Julie has an easy candour, realistic perspectives and incredible ability to help me to see things differently, uncover my strengths and blind spots, reflect on these and take simple steps to improve. I can highly recommend Julie's coaching to any executive looking to reach their full potential and excel in their role, no matter how long they have been at it!'

– R Mowthorpe, Customer Service Director

'Every step of the way, Julie partnered with me to double, then triple, the size and turnover of my business. She was my unwavering support through the roller-coaster of entrepreneurial life. Julie's infectious positivity and vibrant personality have been my compass, keeping me on the path to success, making me accountable, and always striving for new heights.'

– H Haines, Director

'Julie's program gave me some profound insights into my strengths as a leader, mindset to focus on, and framework to plan for the future.'

– A Payne, Sales Executive

'Julie's programs have given me the skills to become more self-aware in both a personal and professional capacity and challenge myself to be the leader I aspire to be, and she offers practical advice and strategies to be able to set and achieve this goal.'

– A Deisio, Broker Manager

www.ingramcontent.com/pod-product-compliance
Ingram Content Group UK Ltd.
Pitfield, Milton Keynes, MK11 3LW, UK
UKHW040642060526
12295UKWH00010B/31